GW01606809

The Incorrigibles:

Perspectives on Disability Visual Arts in the 20th and 21st Centuries

DASH is a disability-led visual arts organisation, set up in 1992, with its origins in the political activism of the Disabled People's and Disability Arts Movements of the 1970s and 1980s. We see Disability Arts as made by Disabled people, reflecting their experience of Disability.

Disability Art has been – and is today – a dynamic and powerful way to raise wider awareness of Disabled people's creativity and to spread understanding of the lack of accessibility, poor representation, general disrespect and lack of recognition they still face in our institutions and in wider society.

DASH is committed to the Social Model of Disability – the idea that people are Disabled not by any impairments they may have, but by negative attitudes in wider society and deliberate or unintentional institutional discrimination.

The current climate of economic austerity has led to ever more drastic cuts to the benefits and services on which many, including Disabled artists, depend, increasing the discrimination they face in their personal and professional lives.

This book is a celebration of recognition and belief – recognition that the significant and inspirational lives and work of Disabled artists make a profound difference to all of us, and belief that their work will continue to reflect the experience of Disabled people in ways that, in Tony Heaton's words, 'make trouble, (and) challenge injustice, prejudice and disablism'.

It is a joyful celebration of Disability Arts as both a key part of and also distinct from mainstream art; as a challenge to our perceptions about the meanings and uses of 'Art', and as a positive force for changing disabling attitudes towards Disabled people.

ISBN 978-1-907796-19-7

Compiled and edited by DASH

DASH
5 Belmont
Shrewsbury
Shropshire
SY1 1TE
+44 (0)1743 272939
www.dasharts.org

First published in 2016 by
mac birmingham
Cannon Hill Park
Birmingham B12 9QH
+44 (0)121 446 3232
www.macbirmingham.co.uk

Distributed by Cornerhouse Publications
70 Oxford Street
Manchester, M1 5NH
+44 (0) 161 200 1503
www.cornerhouse.org

Contents

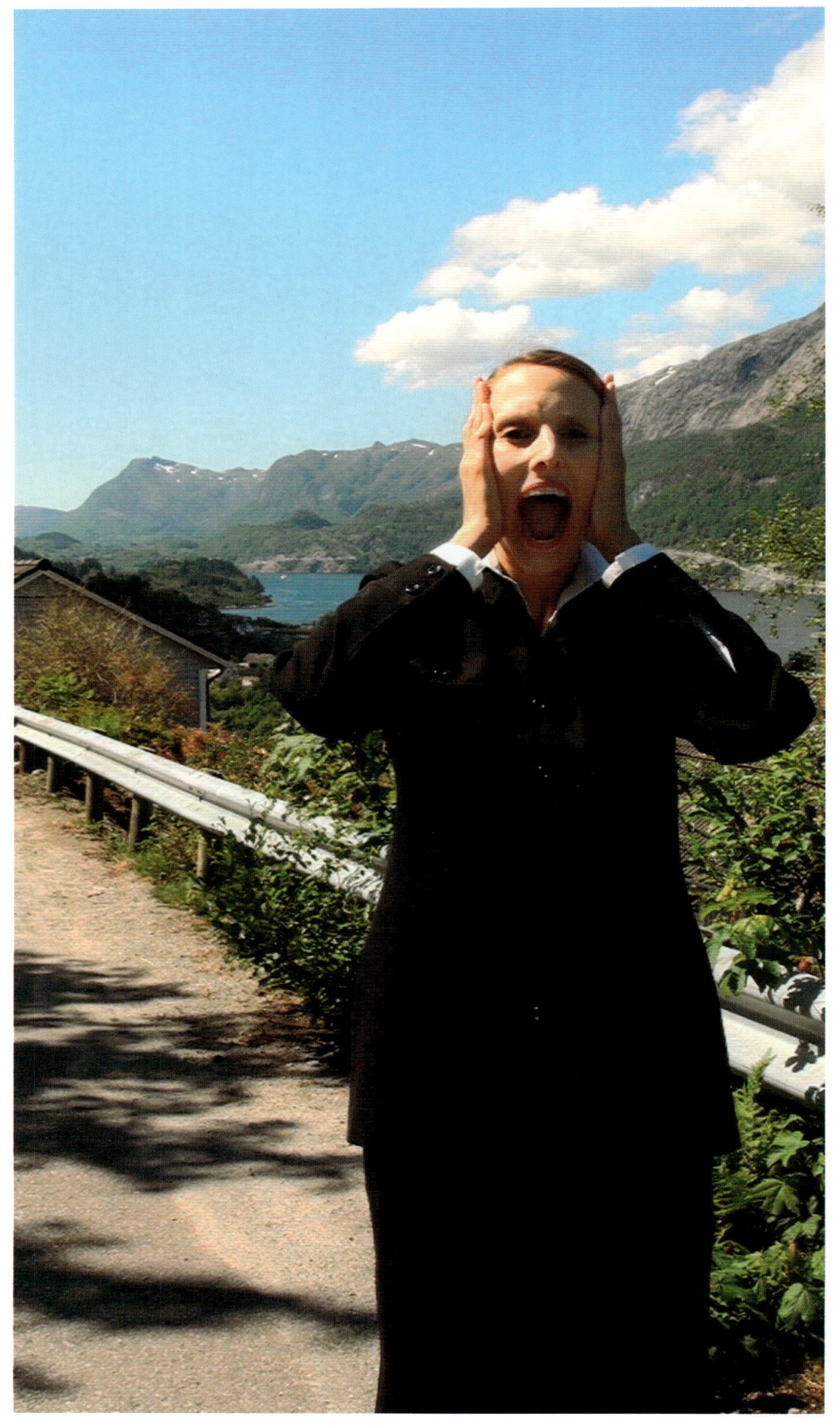

Incorrigible –
(of a person or their behaviour) not able to be changed or reformed

Adrian Plant & Tanya Raabe-Webber

The drive to produce this book grew out of issues raised within two of DASH's recent projects:

Awkward Bastards[1] took place in March 2015, the first in a series of conferences bringing together an array of speakers – including historians, curators and artists – to discuss a wide range of 'diversity' issues.

One recurring theme within the conference was around the decision, both historically and now, to self-identify (or not) as a 'Disabled' or 'black' or 'queer' artist. The positive and negative implications of doing so, and what these implications still tell us about the machinations and prejudices of mainstream cultural organisations, remains an ongoing important political debate as well as a deeply personal dilemma for artists.

Cultivate[2] is a bespoke mentoring project for up and coming Disabled visual artists.

As mentors within the project we became acutely aware that new and emerging Disabled artists were often unaware of the history and current context for potentially aligning their practice, aspirations and identity as artists within a wider 'Disability Arts movement'. They were also often unaware of the work and range of current Disability Arts organisations and the support and resources available to them through these channels.

We hope that this book provides the reader – Disabled or non-disabled, arts professional or generalist, community or social care worker or disability activist – with greater insight and confidence to engage with these issues, and that new dialogues will emerge as a result.

The stories and artwork in this book unite the artists and demonstrate the strong vibrant genre that is progressive and inspirational to an emerging Disability Arts landscape. We are indebted to all the artists who responded with such openness, honesty and generosity of spirit.

This book is not just about Disability Arts and culture, it is a book about artists being artists, it is about a celebration of difference, it is about the will to survive as artists, it is about humanity, it is about the fact that art unites us all as human beings and that Disability Art is here and now!

We hope that *The Incorrigibles* will provide a valuable contribution at this significant and fundamental point in the history of Disability Art and culture. Recognising and understanding the history of Disabled artists in the past and their position in the present will be the basis of generating new and more enlightened practices in the future.

left: Anna Berndtson, *Nations – Norway 1*, Video Loop 9:16, Stereo, 6 min 27 seconds, 2012. Photograph Anna Berndtson

1 www.dasharts.org/projects/awkward-bastards.html

2 www.dasharts.org/projects/cultivate.html

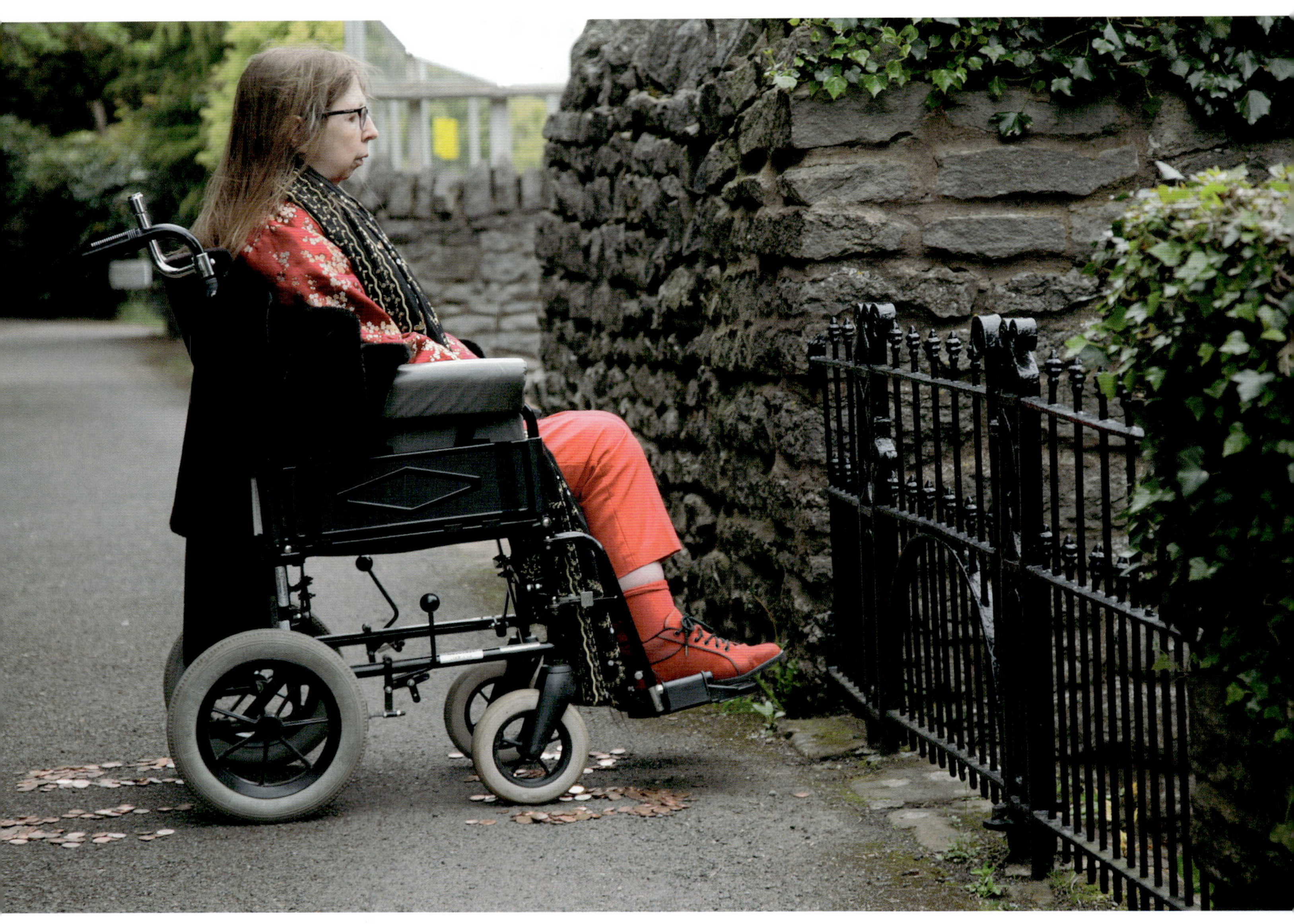

Foreword

Darren Henley OBE, Chief Executive, Arts Council England

The Incorrigibles is a necessary and welcome celebration of the Disability Arts movement, chronicling the contribution that Disabled artists have made to the arts and cultural life of England.

It's important that the stories of these artists are shared and that their work is recognised for its excellence and its impact on artistic, political and social discourse.

I'm delighted that Arts Council England has been able to support the publication of this book. It is an invaluable resource. It will not only raise the profile and reach of the artists featured in the publication, but it will also encourage curators, programmers and arts leaders to research and reach out to the many talented artists that could not be featured.

The work of Disabled artists is now more prominent than ever before. Public awareness has been fuelled in no small part by the success of the London Cultural Olympiad in 2012, which provided a global showcase for the amazing talent and creativity we have in England. The Unlimited programme continues to build on the legacy of the London games through a biennial festival programme at the Southbank Centre and an arts commissioning fund that has supported the development of new work by artists including Jess Thoms, Liz Carr, Aaron Williamson and Noëmi Lakmaier.

left: *The Route Taken*, Ann Whitehurst, live art performance for M21, an Unlimited commission, produced by DASH and LADA. Much Wenlock, 2012. Photograph Richard Foot

Diversity must be seen as an opportunity to refresh and replenish our artistic practice. It belongs at the centre of our artistic discourse where it can shape our programming, commissioning and curatorial decisions and ensure that the work in our theatres, galleries and museums reflects the true diversity of society. We must all make the Creative Case for Diversity.

I believe in the power of creativity to transform lives and change our world for the better. I'm committed to challenging and changing attitudes that prevent the arts from being for everyone, everywhere. There should be no barrier to any artist wishing to realise their creative ambitions. It is vital that the Arts Council continues to empower all artists to create work that excites, provokes, challenges and makes us pause for reflection – as does the work you can read about here.

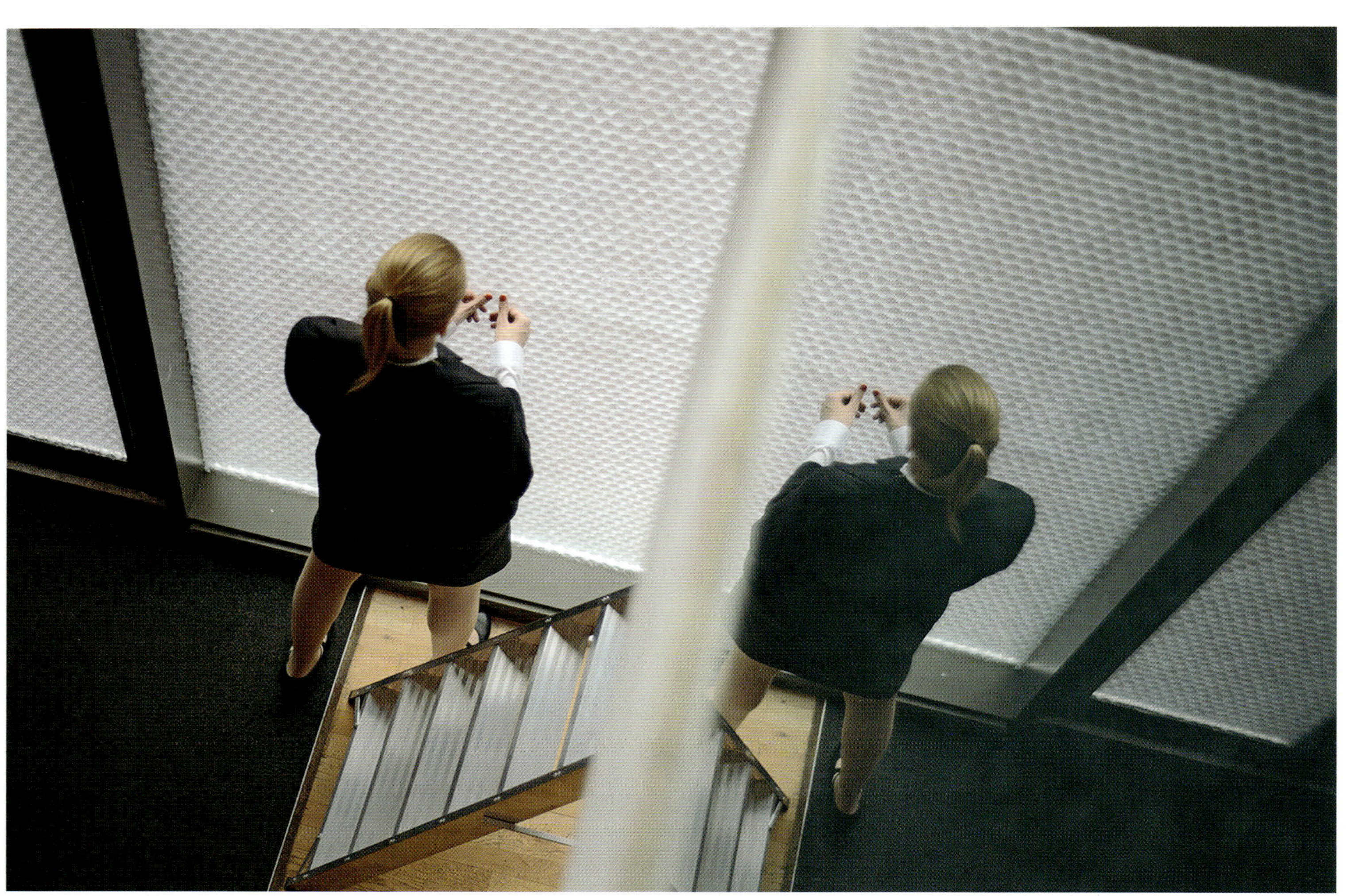

In Praise of Awkwardness

Disability, diversity and the institutional gatekeepers of the mainstream

Craig Ashley

On Thursday 12 March 2015 the eagerly anticipated *Awkward Bastards* symposium arrived at mac Birmingham. Commissioned by the Disability Arts organisation DASH to rethink ideas around diversity, the event took place in mac's main theatre auditorium with accompanying exhibitions and performances happening across the busy public spaces and galleries of the arts centre. With contributions from artists, academics, curators and historians, the programme explored different perspectives on the current state of Disability Arts, and the wider subject of diversity in the mainstream.

In planning the symposium with my co-organiser and collaborator Mike Layward, Artistic Director at DASH, we set about foregrounding a conversation about *what* constitutes the mainstream, and *how* it is constituted in the realm of the arts and culture. We talked at length about the absence of Disability Arts from the institutionally-shaped canon of artistic movements, and the problems with defining oneself as a Disabled artist – the perceived challenges such an association might present, and the possible barriers that may inadvertently be put in place.

At the same time, I was developing a retrospective exhibition of the work of the Manchester-based artist Qasim Riza Shaheen, which showed at mac in the autumn of 2014. The curatorial approach explored 'awkwardness' as an alternative critical framework in which to situate a body of work that had been largely classified and typecast as queer. Awkwardness presented an opportunity to readdress the artist's work without the baggage of a highly loaded term, and to consider it more in relation to an engagement with the audience – a difficult transaction or encounter within the mainstream, rather than a limited and unchallenging position outside of it.

Awkwardness therefore appealed as an alternative starting point for a symposium tasked with rethinking ideas around diversity. This shift or transference of focus, from the difference or impairment of the artist to the audience and the passively observed conventions of the mainstream arts experience, was a critical point to locate in the debate. The social quality of awkwardness seemed to us to be readily aligned with the Social Model of Disability – a recognition that disability is an unhelpful construct of society, rather than an objective diagnosis of psychological, physical or sensory ability relative to the external world in which we live. Extended to the wider territory of diversity in the arts, and appropriated as a social model for the purpose of this discussion, awkwardness provided the neutral ground upon which to begin a new conversation, one

left: Anna Berndtson, *Self Stress Relief*, for *Disrupted* mac Birmingham 12th March 2015. Photographer Hannah Levy

that reflected upon and scrutinised the societally-defined context of the arts environment, alongside the concerns of artists that were centred largely on identity, self-definition and classification.

We felt there was a question around legitimacy that also needed to be framed as part of the conversation, to acknowledge the historical context of exclusion and subsequent civil rights action in Britain during the post-war period. In his appropriately provocative symposium title, *Awkward Bastards*, Mike Layward referenced legitimacy, or rather a perception that groups or individuals operating outside of the mainstream were considered in some way illegitimate, or otherwise implicated as bastards by the establishment.

Our public-facing arts organisations and agencies, acting as intermediaries between the artist and the audience, tend also to be the institutional gatekeepers, taste-makers and trendsetters with a significant and collective influence upon the mainstream. Is it possible, we wondered, to dispel the perceived correlation between legitimacy and the mainstream, or is it necessary to continue to broaden the mainstream to include the last of the outsiders?

For those who had travelled to attend *Awkward Bastards* from across the UK, as well as the many viewers online who had tuned in to receive the live broadcast, there were perhaps no real surprises amongst the evidence and experiences presented throughout the day. Speakers echoed time and again the widely-held view that there is still much work to be done in creating equitable opportunities around leadership and access in the arts, as indeed there is across society more generally.

However, despite the familiar and persisting challenges associated with diversity in the cultural industries, the overarching tone of the symposium was a hopeful one. A shared sense of optimism accompanied the difficult conversations about representation and inclusion, and mainstream arts organisations were positively acknowledged on the whole for continuing their work in beginning to shift the institutional ground in relation to matters of gender, race, class and disability. Slow though it may be, progress was happening and seen to be happening on a number of fronts.

Referred to frequently on the day was Arts Council England's Creative Case for Diversity, an initiative that speaks about the need for diversity in the mainstream. The Creative Case, the shortened name by which it has become known, has located diversity as a strategic goal for each of the 684 arts organisations currently in receipt of regular funding – the National Portfolio Organisations and Major Partner Museums. Between 2015 and 2018, diversity is firmly cited by the Arts Council as 'a key issue in relation to the programming and audiences, leadership and workforce of all our funded organisations.'[1]

In the introduction to her short presentation about her own personal history of diversity in the arts, connected to the Blk Art Group and the Black Arts Movement in the UK, the artist and curator Marlene Smith declared her belief in revolution and made the following provocation: 'It is an open secret that our cultural infrastructure was founded upon and still rests on a tower of elitism. In the UK we cling for dear

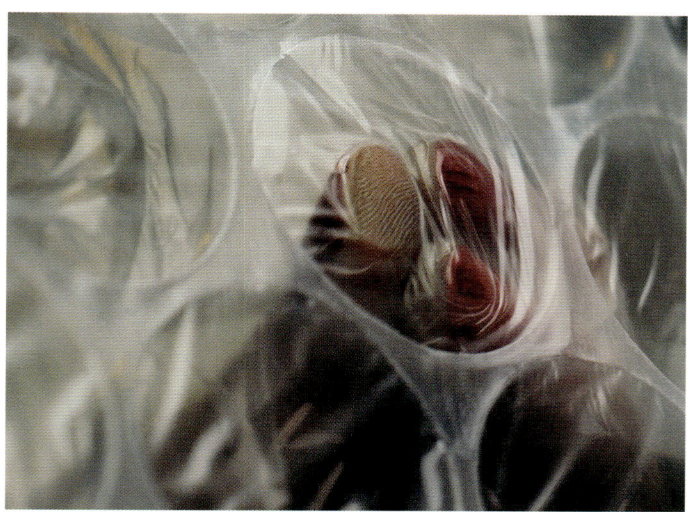

Anna Berndtson, *Self Stress Relief* (detail)

life to the old order, pay lip service to the notion of change and quake in our boots at the thought and consequences of revolution.'[2]

Whether the Creative Case will be effective in helping to bring about a revolution, and demolish the 'elitist tower', remains to be seen. Clearly it will take some time to measure the impact of the current endeavours in effecting change, and navigate the resistance that it will face. Nevertheless, the determination of the Arts Council and others to address diversity at a national and strategic level is surely a good thing. From the artists and the artworks commissioned, to staff and the contractors employed, there appears now to be a concerted effort to move beyond a superficial addressing of diversity – a move away from the purely project-based model that would often see activity delivered by and for 'diverse groups' in isolation, to an earnest dialogue that recognises the value of a wider set of perspectives and cultural experiences as integral and mutually beneficial.

This is perhaps an overly optimistic note on which to end. Events such as *Awkward Bastards* all too often conclude in a positive manner with groups of likeminded people agreeing cheerfully that the world is a slightly better place than it was at the beginning of the day. As a sector and as a society, we do need to be watchful and vigilant, to be certain that progress continues to be made and also to ensure that the intricacies and complexities of culture – not just its reductive facets and features – are acknowledged, respected and made visible. The sentiment of the Japanese author and novelist Jun'ichirō Tanizaki resonates here. In his 1933 essay In Praise of Shadows[3], the reader is invited to consider the nuanced qualities between light and darkness, and to appreciate the subtleties within the shade. While these passive observations allow us to monitor change from a distance, there is a need for activism and intervention too – and here the merits of awkwardness as a catalyst for change should be recognised and applauded. By taking a position of awkwardness, we are empowered to ask difficult questions, to challenge the legitimate ground where it is assumed or outmoded, and to propose alternative territories for the mainstream.

1 Arts Council England. 2014. *Creative Case for Diversity 2015–18.* [Online]. [Accessed 2 June 2016]. Available from: http://www.artscouncil.org.uk/

2 Smith, M. 2015. *Rethinking Diversity.* [Online]. 12 March, mac Birmingham. Awkward Bastards symposium. DASH and mac Birmingham. [Accessed 2 June 2016]. Available from: https://www.youtube.com/watch?v=2F-uw0yJPpc

3 Tanizaki, J. 1933. *In Praise of Shadows.* London: Vintage Classics.

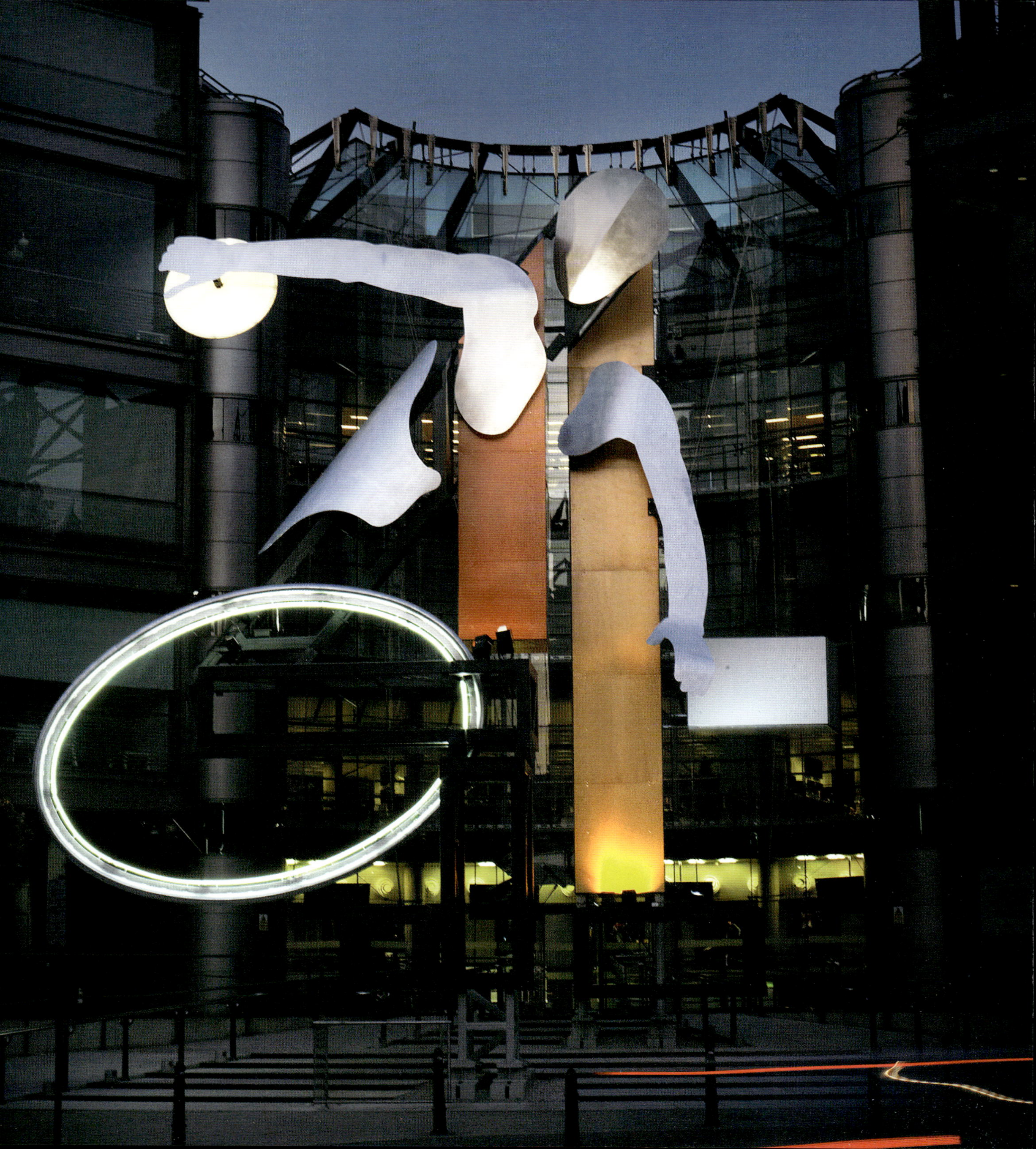

Different Shoes

Tony Heaton OBE

A quote from the travel writer Bill Bryson[1] might be a strange place to begin an essay that sketches out something of the history of Disability Arts, but bear with me.

Bryson introduces us to a study of national inventiveness produced by Japan's Ministry of International Trade and Industry, which concluded that in the modern era, Britain has produced 55 per cent of all the world's 'significant inventions', against 22 per cent for America and 6 per cent for Japan. This is an astonishing proportion and amongst this innovation we must count Disability Arts. It is a genre conceived in the UK, is inextricably linked to the Disability Rights movement and it grew out of a time when Disabled people in the UK were questioning the perceived view that disability was an issue for the medical, health and social services, rather than a human rights issue and therefore something we could all of us address in removing barriers and challenging prejudice and discrimination.

It is difficult to pin down the actual birth of this term 'Disability Arts' and its context but as *Shape*[2] celebrates its 40th anniversary this year, 2016, it is probably reasonable to consider that it was around the mid-1970s.

left: Tony Heaton, *Monument to the Unintended Performer*, steel, neon, (gold, silver, bronze lacquer), 15.24m, 2012 Paralympic Games, installation on the BIG 4 outside Channel 4 TV Broadcasting Head Office, London. Technical support FreeState. Photograph Dave King

The National Disability Arts Collection and Archive[3] (NDACA), a project led by *Shape* and funded by the Heritage Lottery Fund, in embryo for some years and launched coincidently this year, will doubtless unearth some documentary evidence that may shed light on the birth of Disability Arts, or some long forgotten event where this term was coined, but let's not worry about it.

Disability Art exists and I for one feel better and stronger in knowing this.

The politicisation of disability and the radical nature of much of the art of that historical time fused together and this, coupled with the Social Model of Disability proposed by Mike Oliver and Vic Finkelstein, was potent and liberating for many Disabled people.

A vanguard fought to force changes; to the built environment, goods and services and discriminatory attitudes to Disabled people and this change started to happen. It challenged local authorities and hegemony and built positive relationships with allies who recognised that we quite rightly wanted civil rights and who supported this struggle to legislation. This of course meant demanding access to art galleries, museums and theatres and by that we meant access through the front door.

Many Disabled artists have told me that whilst at art college they were dissuaded from looking at issues relating to their impairment or their Disability identity, that this was not something worth developing as part of their practice if they wanted a successful career. This is a form of oppression and one that I was fortunate not to face; on the contrary, the Fellow in Sculpture at my university observed that my footprints in the sand were different from the rest of the students and that this might be something to investigate as part of my practice. I did – and started making my own disability artwork back then in the 1980s. I just didn't realise at that time that there was something called 'Disability Arts' and that it was just beginning to happen.

I exhibited my work and was approached by *North West Shape* who provided me with opportunities and a network. Coincidently at this time, 1986, the London Disability Arts Forum (LDAF) was founded and Disability Arts in London (DAiL) magazine was established to highlight, promote and review the work of organisations such as *Shape*, *Graeae*[4] and *Heart n Soul*[5], including the creative work of individual Disabled people.

I met and exhibited with others from what might be termed the first wave of Disabled visual artists in an LDAF promoted show at the Diorama Gallery, London, called *'Out of Ourselves'* with Nancy Willis, Trevor Landell, Lucy Jones, who are all still creating work, and Adam Reynolds.

Adam was an exceptional sculptor who worked in a range of materials including scrap, lead, copper and found objects, chosen deliberately to confront the viewer to reconsider the value and beauty of materials rejected and overlooked. This he described as being: *'founded on my lifelong experience of disability and to challenge the commonplace assumption that this renders life all but useless and without value'.*

He made figurative and abstract works, a number of which are in the Shape Arts Collection. (Adam was both a trustee and Chair of *Shape*). Adam stated: *'I am clear that my greatest strengths stem from the fact of being born with muscular dystrophy, apparently my greatest weakness'.*

Adam died in 2005. His obituary was written for the Guardian by Tate Director Sir Nicholas Serota and *Shape* perpetuates his memory through the Adam Reynolds Memorial Bursary (ARMB), an annual bursary aimed at mid-career Disabled artists.

To date the artists Noëmi Lakmaier, Sally Booth, Caroline Cardus, Aaron Williamson, Aaron McPeake, Simon Raven, Carmen Papalia and Çağlar Kimyoncu have undertaken the ARMB in some of the UK's most creative contemporary galleries: the Camden Arts Centre, The Bluecoat Gallery, the BALTIC, Spike Island, the V&A and the New Art Gallery, Walsall. The sculptor Sir Antony Gormley described the ARMB as the most practical and powerful way to continue doing what Adam did to make the possible palpable.

By 1990 there was a proliferation of organisations throughout the UK and Northern Ireland with events and happenings across all art forms. This continued throughout the 1990's, with Disability Arts forums and consortiums and the development of

right: *Great Britain from a Wheelchair,* Tony Heaton, wheelchair components from two condemned ex-ministry wheelchairs, 165cm, 1994. Photographer: Paul Kenny

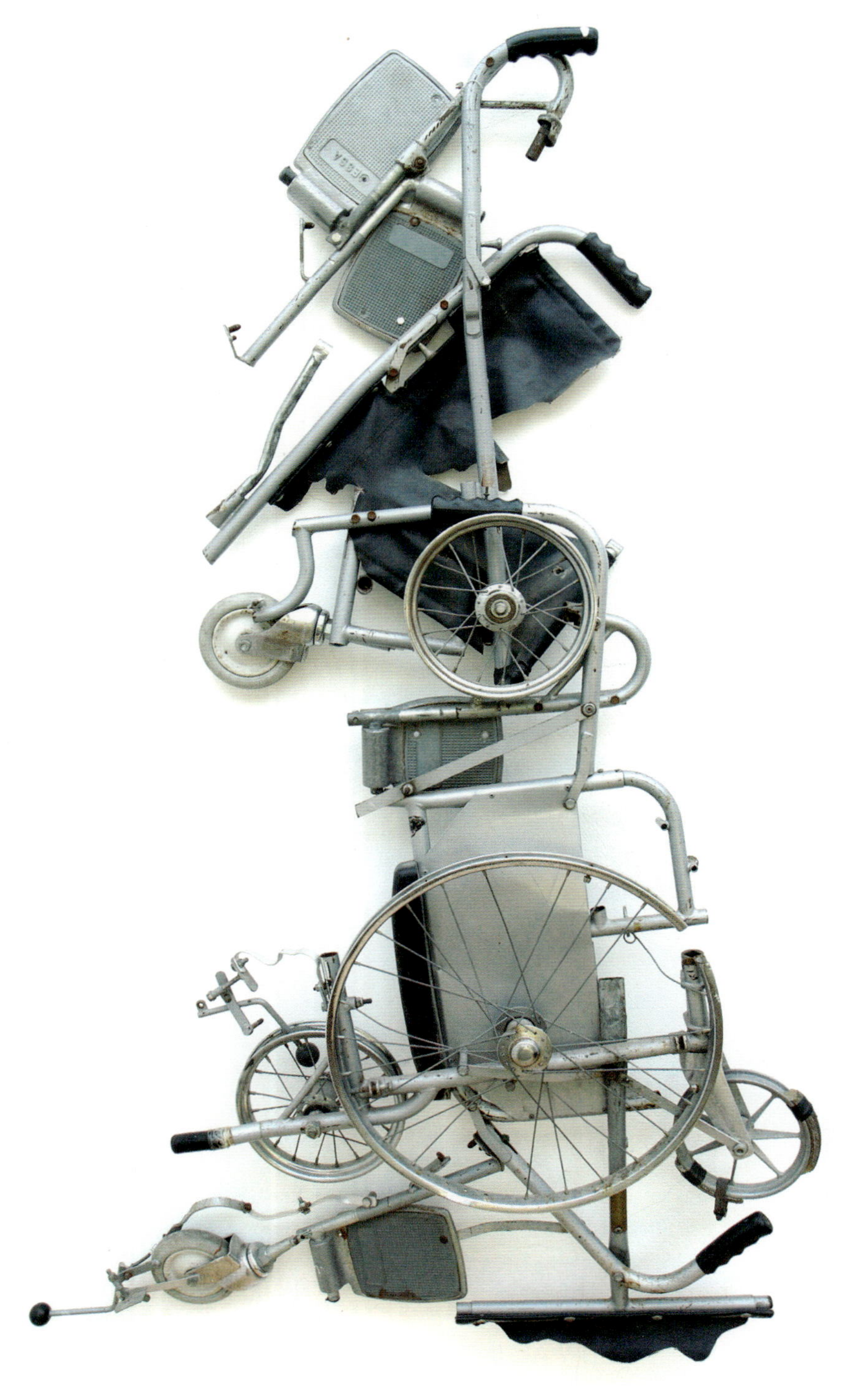

organisations such as DASH in Shropshire and DaDaFest[6] in Liverpool.

The internationally renowned artist Yinka Shonibare MBE said: *'My career in the arts started in 1992 with* Shape. *When I left Goldsmiths College I was looking for opportunities to develop my career.* Shape *offered me my first opportunity to be involved in the arts. What* Shape *does for Disabled artists can make a very big impact on their development. It was certainly the case for me.'*

Now, twenty five years later, this is still happening and the opportunities are greater and the networks are wider – regionally, nationally and internationally. Back then much of this activity and development was reported through the pages of DAiL Magazine[7] or DAM Magazine[8]: without both these publications, much of the history of Disability Arts would be lost. Editors Sian Vasey, Elspeth Morrison, Kit Wells and Colin Hambrook became the guardians and Colin Hambrook went on to launch the digital journal DAO[9] (Disability Arts Online) in 2002 and has been for over twenty years at the forefront of the commentary on Disability Arts.

Also in 2002 the Faith House Gallery was constructed at Holton Lee in Dorset[10] where I was Director. This award-winning building was the first fully accessible gallery space dedicated to showing and promoting the work of Disabled artists. This was closely followed by a suite of artists' studios and many of the artists from this first wave had work exhibited and many new Disabled artists had opportunities, often for the first time, to show work. The gallery was opened with a performance from Signdance Collective – Julie McNamara, Allan Sutherland, Adam Reynolds, Aidan Shingler, Tanya Raabe-Webber, Rachel Gadsden, Sally Booth, Sue Austin and many more artists performed, exhibited or made work there.

These artists continue to inspire and attract new waves of artists and allies who see the value, the truly unique stories and who want to support and promote our work.

Currently *Shape* and *Artsadmin*[11] are delivery partners for Unlimited[12], Unlimited International and Unlimited Impact, funded by the Arts Council, Creative Scotland, the Spirit of 2012 and Arts Council Wales. Initiatives such as these ensure that Disability Arts and work by Disabled artists will be seen by wider audiences than those who pioneered the genre; this is inevitable, and some of the artists from those earlier times continue to develop work through Unlimited including Aaron Williamson, Katherine Araniello, Bobby Baker and Kaite O'Reilly.

The widely held definition of Disability Arts is: *Art made by Disabled artists that is informed by or reflects the personal* ***experience*** *of disability.*

It is not an aberration or a phase; it is not an apprenticeship into the mainstream (whatever that is). It is not a ghetto; it is a genre rich with the most audacious, moving, funny, thought-provoking, subversive, life-changing work. That this is so is witnessed by the fact that many of those, then, young artists, writers, performers and creatives are still today making work and making trouble, challenging injustice, prejudice and disablism.

Their histories and past trailblazing can be seen in the Chronology of Disability Arts[13], created by the poet, writer and disability historian Allan Sutherland who was commissioned in the early days of the visioning for NDACA to provide a tool to understanding how this disability culture came about.

Disability Arts has been described as the last *'avant-garde'* and remains so.

In a world where much contemporary art is dull and conventional, conservative and dead, we should celebrate the existence of Disability Arts.

That curators and critics fail to see beyond the phenomena of difference or disability – by that I mean impairment – means they obsess with the idea of the overcoming of our impairments. When they have written about that, they then struggle to say anything meaningful about the work we do because they come from such a different place that they are often unable to appropriate the work, having neither the experience nor vocabulary to discuss it. This deficit is an issue and crucial because we really do need many more Disabled people as curators and critics to help us to develop and evaluate the work.

Perhaps the fact that Disability Arts is not valued is because Disabled people are not valued; but Disabled people will always be present in society, both as intended and unintended performers and artists. They will always explore themselves, their experience, how they see the world and how the world sees them. Artists who are, or who become Disabled will indubitably do this and make creative work as a result, thus perpetuating this world we call Disability Arts.

It is inevitable and it's spreading out across the world, you can't stop it.

1 Bill Bryson, *The Road to Little Dribbling*, Penguin Random House UK, 2015 p195

2 www.shapearts.org.uk

3 www.ndaca.org.uk

4 www.graeae.org

5 www.heartnsoul.co.uk

6 www.dadafest.co.uk

7 www.ndaca.org.uk/NDACA-Dail

8 www.digital-disability.com/heritage/publications/dam-disability-arts-magazine

9 www.disabilityartsonline.org.uk

10 www.holtonlee.org

11 www.artsadmin.co.uk

12 www.weareunlimited.org.uk

13 www.disabilityartsonline.org.uk/Chronology_of_Disability_Arts

The Incorrigibles:

Fourteen selected artists were asked send in images of their work and asked to respond to the questions below, with the aim of providing inspiration and advice for the readers of this book.

The results on the next fifty six pages are poignant, fascinating, expressive and of incredible quality.

A What/who inspired you to want to become an artist?

B What were the main personal challenges you faced during your early career as an artist, and what strategies did you develop to overcome them?

C As an established/respected artist can you reflect on your relationship to the so-called 'mainstream' museum and art worlds?

D In what ways has the existence of the 'Disability Art movement' helped or hindered your career development?

E Tanya Raabe-Webber identifies herself to be a Disabled Artist, borne out of the Disability Arts movement. How do you choose to define yourself as an artist and why?

F What advice would you consider most vital to give to an emerging Disabled Artist and why?

Jon Adams

A: I was having my portrait drawn and was asked what I was going to be when I grew up and I replied I was going to be an artist. I was six at the time and said this because that's how I felt; I hadn't thought about it, it just felt the right thing and I don't know whether I've really fulfilled that desire until now. I was always being creative; then at school, aged 10, I had a picture torn up in front of the class by a teacher who said I'd never be anything, because I couldn't spell my name. This is why I never went to art college and studied geology instead, which was another love of mine.

While I was waiting to do a PhD in sharks I worked part time at the Barbican Art Centre and it was there that I first experienced synaesthesia in response to an artist's paintings, and realised that I was going the wrong way and needed to be that artist I said I would be at six. That artist was Asger Jorn. As they were unwrapping his pictures I could hear and taste them, and that made me turn back and walk the path to become the artist I am now. I spent 30 years drawing other people's pictures as a book illustrator but I now tend to use all my experiences in the socially engaged or contemporary work I make, including my geological learning and my autistic way of viewing the world.

B: I always knew I was different. I had a lot of trouble with spelling but I was never diagnosed at school or university as either dyslexic or autistic – that came later. The events at school did change me. I've always lived with depression and I've always been quite reclusive; these were the main barriers I faced, it's why I became a book illustrator because I could do most of my work at home and keep out of the way of people. It's people who have always been my kryptonite, who have tried to spoil things and put themselves in the way.

C: I don't consider that I'm disabled by my autism at all, but I do by other people's attitude towards it. I knew that people would tend to upset me so I got round this by getting to know editors and picture editors and I used to go and see them, rather than rely on letters or phone calls, so I knew what exactly was wanted. If you have low self-esteem, when people say they really like your work sometimes it doesn't sink in, and often the main barrier is you... so I've had to learn to overcome that, something I'm still doing.

We are very capable of being very creative we just need the right environment, the right

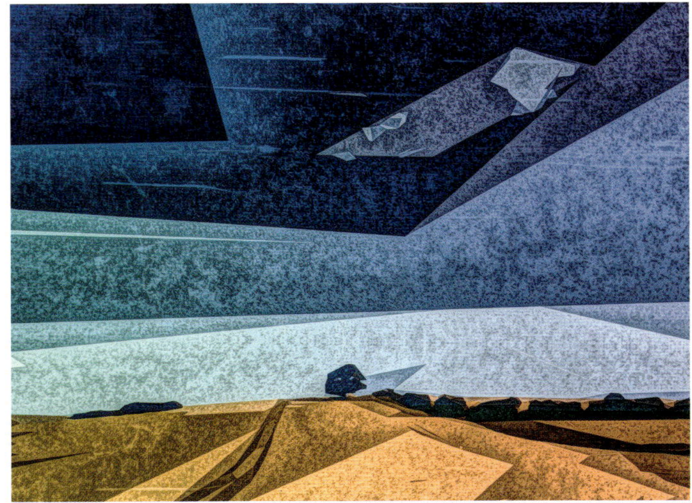

Hill 217 Somerset, digital illustration, 59.5 x 84cm, 2015

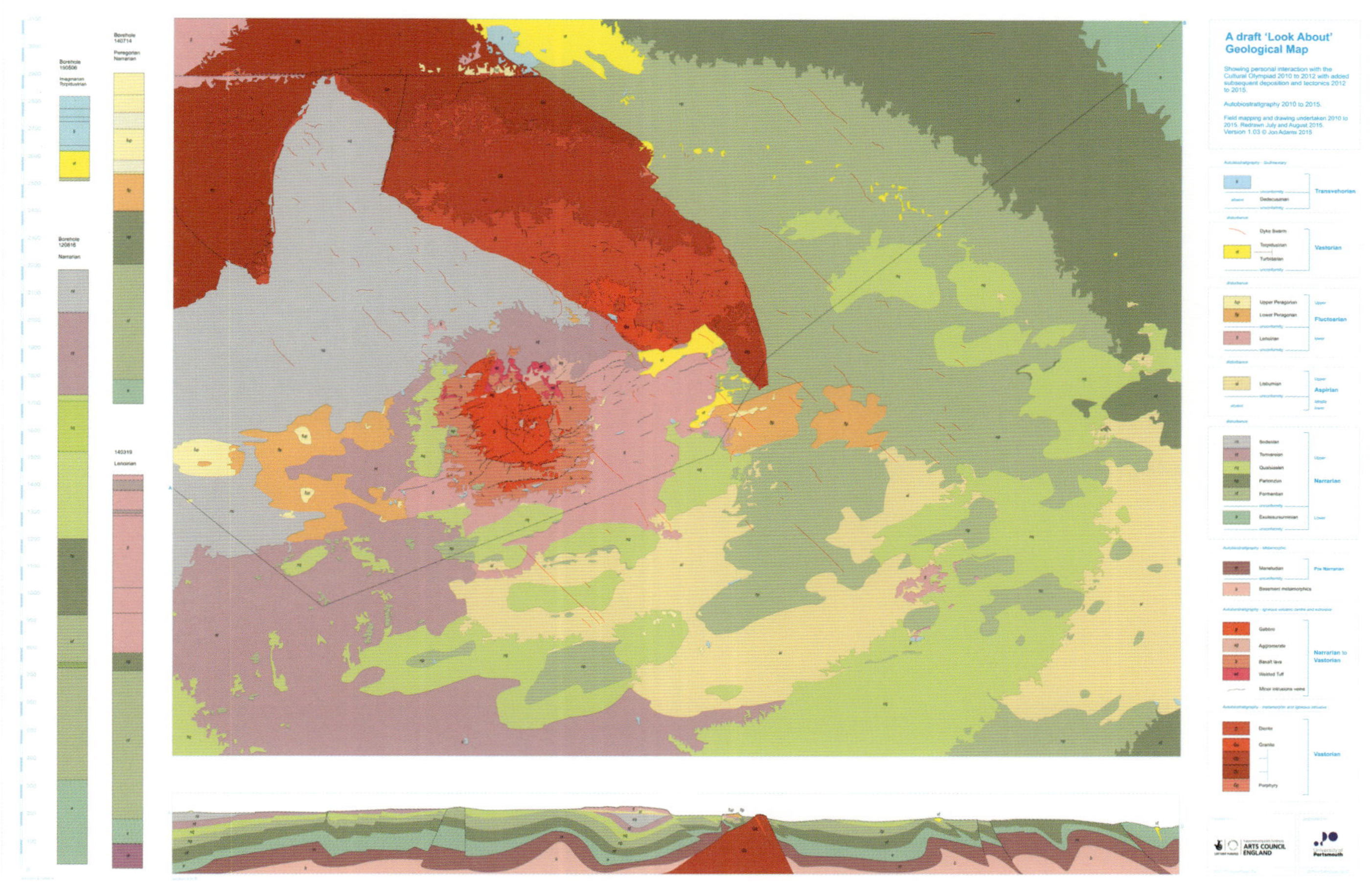

encouragement and understanding. If we don't get this we can end up with severe mental health issues which present as an internal barrier, stopping us from being included.

D: To be honest I've never registered that there is anything other than mainstream; I don't like using the word mainstream as it implies segregation. I've always been an artist who's totally operated within the mainstream, although this has been difficult and I've often needed support to do so. The work should

above: *Look About Geological Map*, digital illustration, 59.5 x 84cm, 2015. Accentuate South East and Arts Council England – Grants for the Arts funded

speak for itself. The arts world is very diverse and who's to say some of the best things don't happen at the edges but it is still part of the mainstream arts world. It's all about how to include people not exclude them; using the word 'mainstream' excludes people.

Autism friendly showings and museum accessibility are really great, but what about

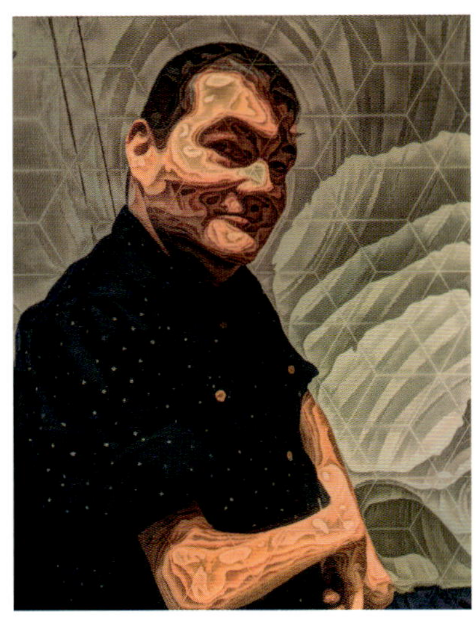

left: *John Kelly Portrait*, digital illustration, 84 x 59.5cm, 2016. Thank you to John Kelly

right: *Margate Chair – Games with the Waterhorse*, digital illustration, 84 x 59.5cm, 2015

neurodivergent artists too? Where's the provision for them to show their work safely? Where museums actually involve autistic people to guide accessibility, like I have been doing with the Imperial War Museum, good things happen for authentic inclusion.

I've always worked in the mainstream and although I consider that I'm disabled by society sometimes, people with hidden abilities (as opposed to hidden disabilities) can be mistreated by both sides of the fence and we walk a very thin line across no man's land which gives us the freedom not to take sides. I have a lot of friends in the Disability Arts movement but I wouldn't say that I'm included, but that's partly my choice.

I have actively been chosen for projects because of my Autism/Aspergers including *'Konfirm'* with The Arts Catalyst, ARC & Professor Simon Baron-Cohen; *'Democracy Street'* with the Houses of Parliament; and *'Valley of Astonishment'* with Sir Peter Brook, a play about synaesthesia & memory.

I don't define myself as a Disabled artist; I don't take that literally. I'm an artist first and yes, I'm an autistic person, I have dyslexia, but it's mainly people who disable me not what I can or can't do – the rules are set by people not by creativity. I'm very happy to say I'm an outsider because the true definition is someone who is untrained and self-taught, which I've done for myself over the years. I think differently, I'm wired differently, I view the world differently, I'm bound to see things that other people can't.

I may be the one in 100 that solves a problem because they're all out front looking at the obvious and I'm tinkering in the back. If you want to see work that is very different, commission people who think differently, but also think differently about the way you commission and treat them; we need parity with other minority groups – we need neurodivergent groups and organisations run by neurodivergent people so we are enabled to get the right support, not the support people imagine we need.

F: My advice would be to always believe in yourself, always believe in what you can do, not what other people tell you you can't do, and if you need support, ask for it. There are lots of people with similar experiences out there who can give you advice and support. Sometimes life can feel very isolating and just to know you're part of a 'tribe', whichever one you feel you belong to, does you good – but whatever you do, make, create, do what you feel in your heart you should be doing, not what other people tell you you should.

http://www.artspace.co.uk/artist.php?artist=71&page_id=21

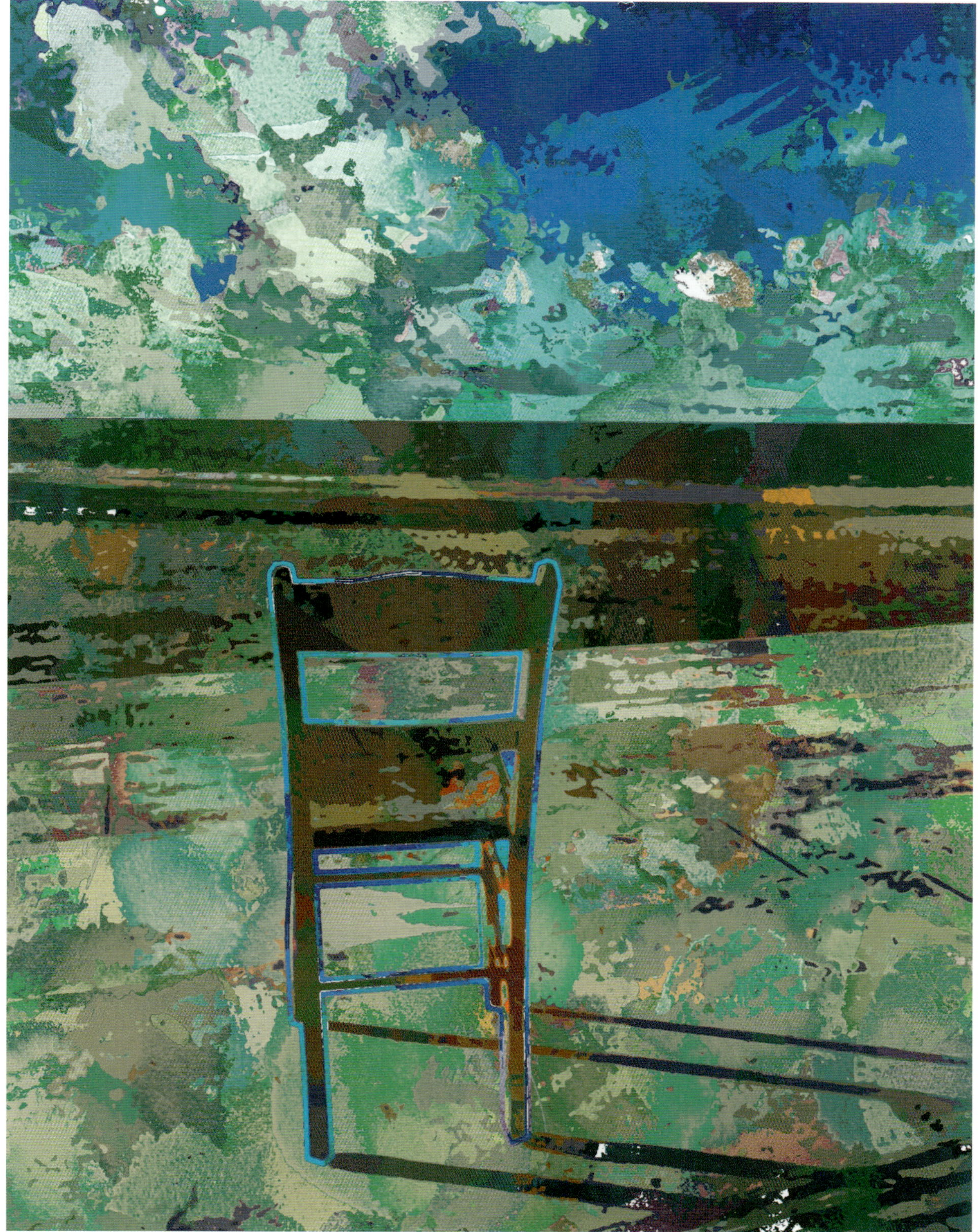

Sue Austin

A: Creativity and the arts have always been a core part of my life. My Aunt, Marianne Unwin (d, 1987), was an artist-printmaker so I grew up surrounded by complex, consummate imagery. As a teenager I entered a room at the Tate filled with Giacometti sculptures. That powerful, visceral experience opened my mind to new ways of seeing the world. Later, a similarly transporting experience occurred on seeing Botticelli's *'Springtime'* and *'Venus Emerging from the Waves'*. The drama, scale and spectacle of those canvases now shape my artistic practice that has emerged in the last 15 years.

B: An interest in the therapeutic power of art underpinned my career in the mental health sector. After becoming a wheelchair user and retiring on ill health grounds, people's reactions completely changed towards me. I realised I'd internalised those responses, changing who I was on a core level. I knew I needed to make new narratives to understand my changed embodiment and reclaim my identity. In response, I remembered those formative

below: *Flying Free*. right: *Glass Fish Pinnacle*, Live Art documented in photograph, 2012. An Unlimited commission. Photograph Norman Lomax

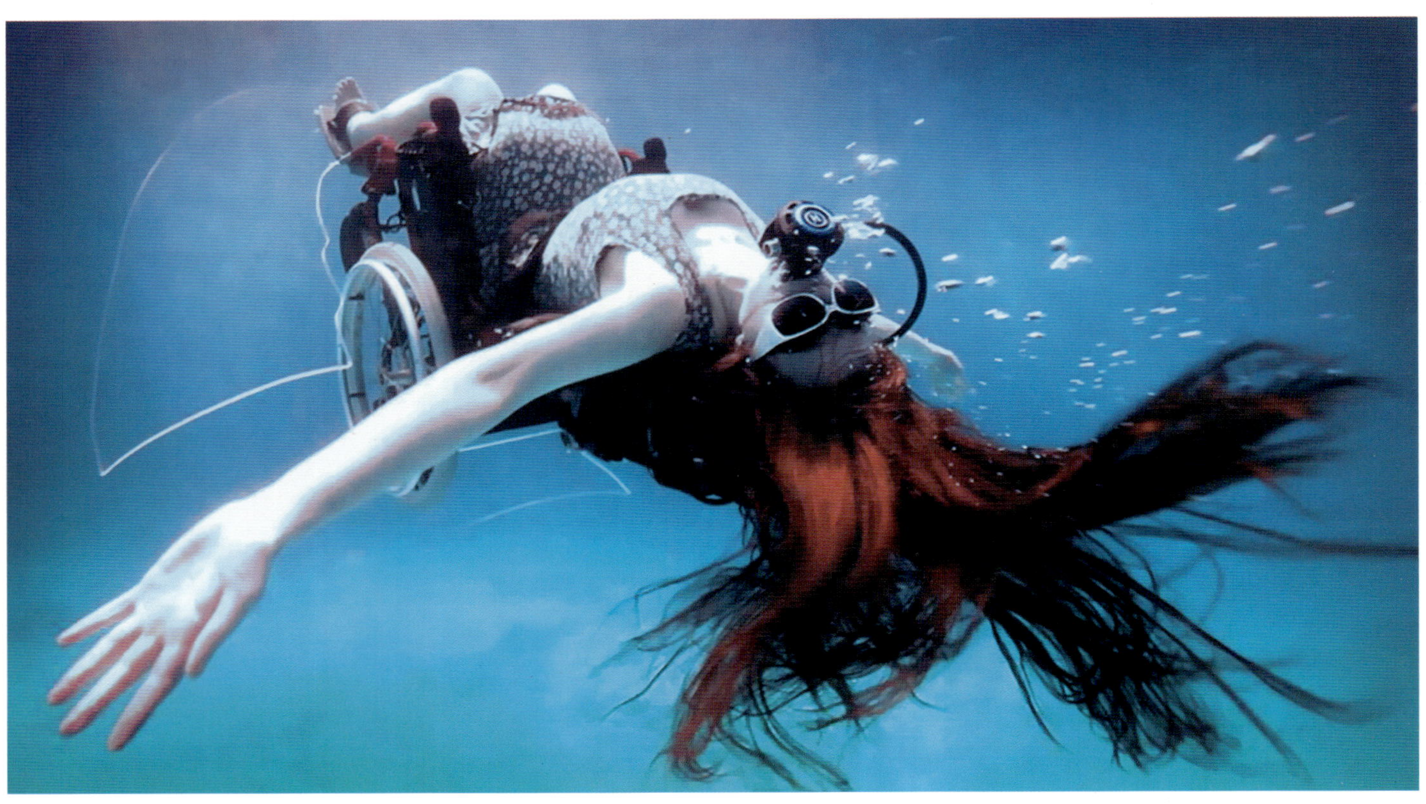

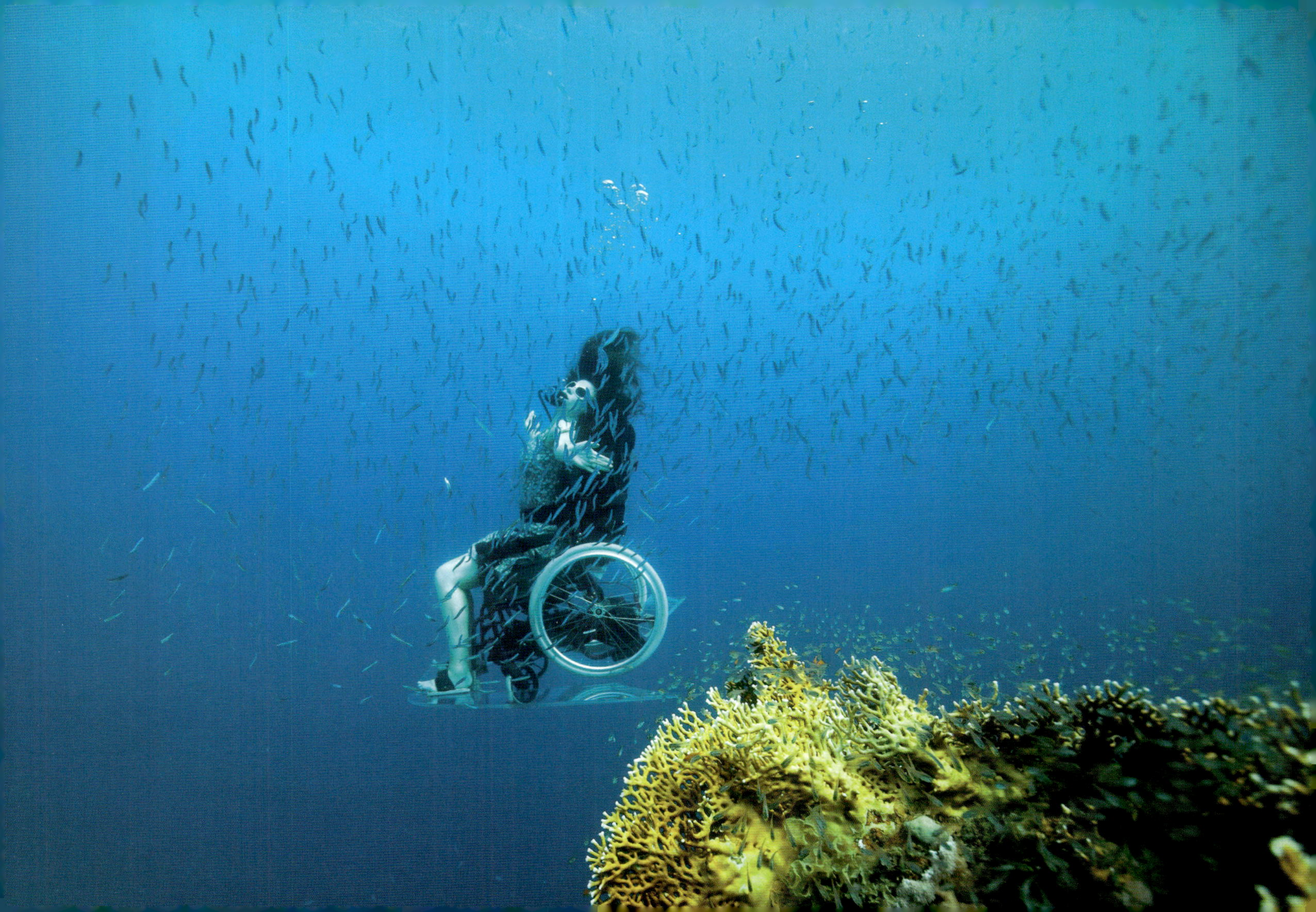

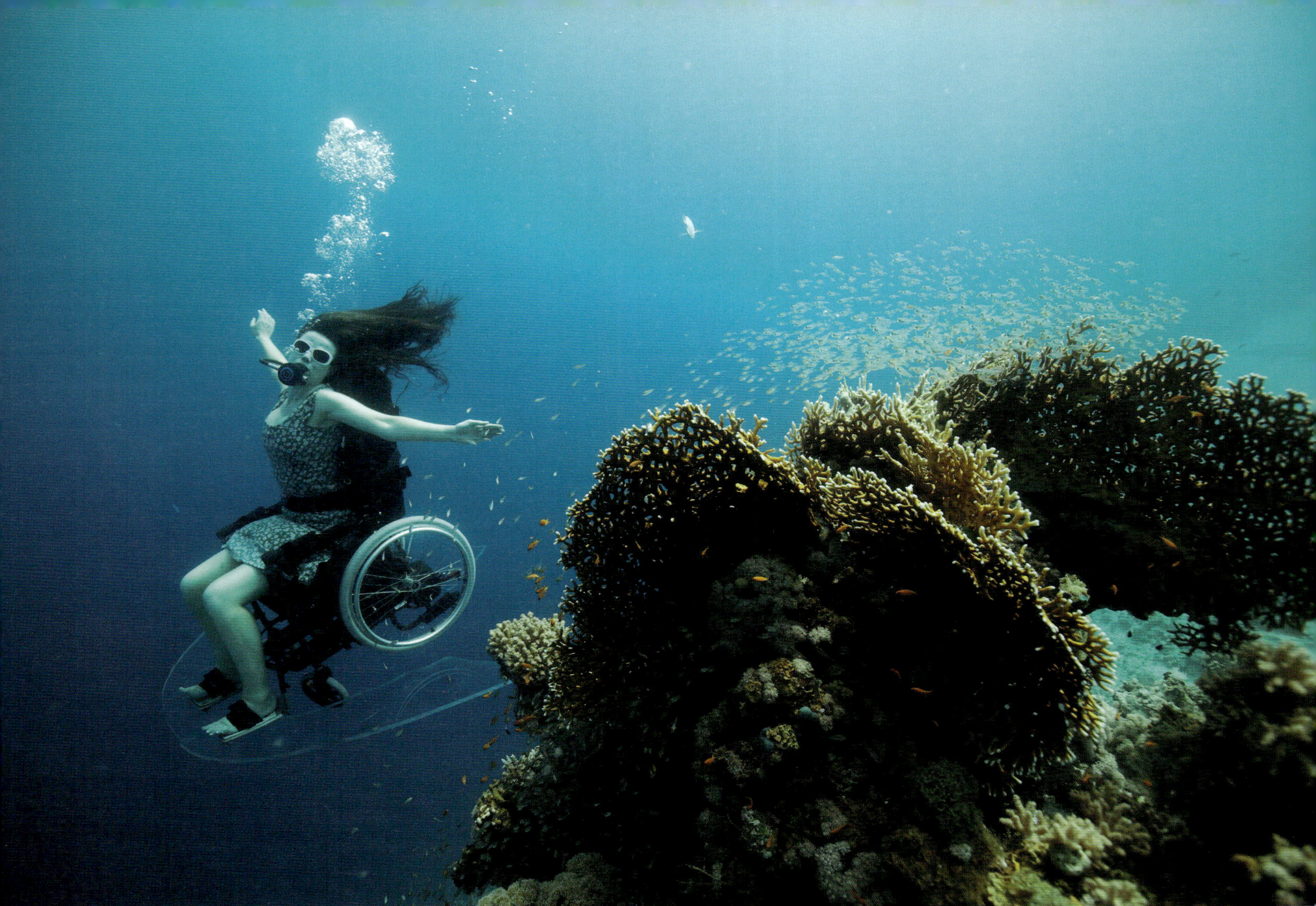

artistic experiences, setting me on a route to achieving those new narratives through developing an artistic practice.

C: It has been interesting to watch the imagery of the underwater wheelchair travel out into the world. Although the work has been exhibited in mainstream arts venues and museums internationally, the primary aim is to open a thinking space, by creating portals or multiple entrances into the artwork so that it can 'ask' questions, whilst leaving space for the audience to generate their own meanings. Therefore all the different places it's been shared are of value in generating that dynamic exchange whether that be the Adelaide Film Festival, NASA, the European Parliament,

above: *Fan Coral Pinnacle*, Live Art documented in photograph, 2012. An Unlimited commission. Photograph Norman Lomax

TED.com, Facebook, Youtube, BBC or the Turbine Hall at Tate Modern.

D: I feel a sense of recognition and shared identity when engaging with Disability Arts that acknowledges the complex realities of the disability experience. Indeed, my practice has been influenced by understanding how Disabled artists have used their practice socially and politically to facilitate change. Performative practices that are underpinned by self-defined theoretical concepts have had a profound impact and helped me understand how being an artist could impact the narratives around disability.

E: I define myself as a multimedia, performance and installation artist with a socially engaged practice that has been shaped and informed by the Disability Arts Movement. I enjoy working with the ambiguities created by varying preconceptions about disability, particularly around the use of wheels to negotiate the world. My practice has been shaped by exposure to the work of other Disabled artists communicating their experiences in rich and complex ways.

F: Working in the context of acquired physical and cognitive impairments has been like emerging into a world shaped by different rules. This has informed my practice and has taken me to places I could never have imagined. I would therefore say *'work with and value your difference, your unique perspective on the world, develop persistence and resilience, learn to tolerate uncertainty and collaborate with people who truly support your work'.*

wearefreewheeling.org.uk
http://www.ted.com/speakers/sue_austin

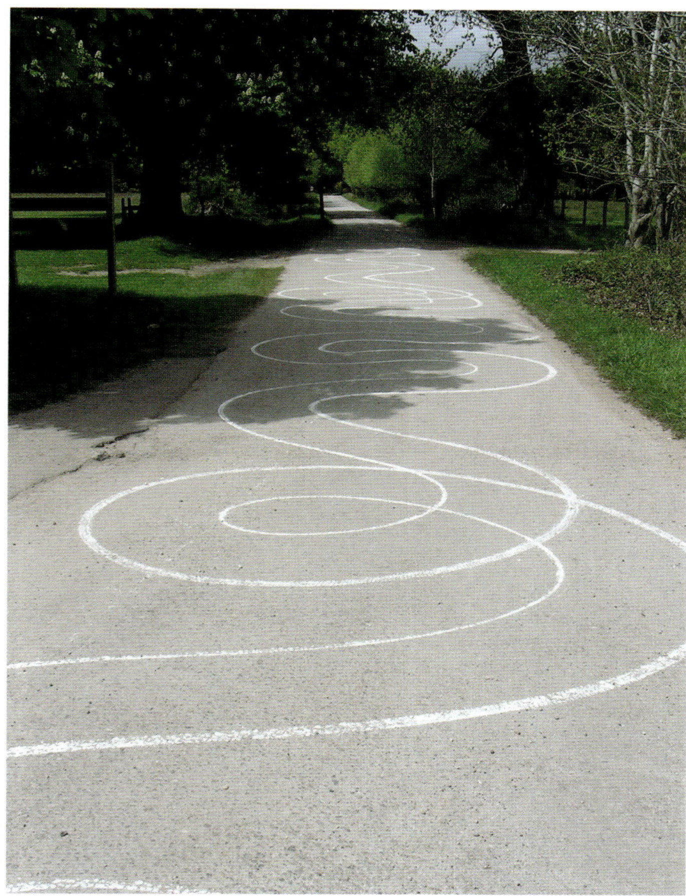

Freewheeling, site specific installation using pitch-marking paint, 2009. Residency and exhibition at Holton Lee, Poole, Dorset. Photograph Sue Austin

Bobby Baker

A: I decided to become an artist when I was 9. This plan took shape when I was really young. My brother and I walked past Sidcup Art School on our way to the park. He told me that naughty, interesting things went on in there, which appealed to me. Definitely more fun than becoming the 'nice nurse' planned by my mother.

Then a great aunt called Dorothy gave me a lesson in painting when I was 9. Her husband had been killed in WW1 so she went to art school, as a way to start her new life. She became a celebrated teacher and her interest in me, and praise for my drawing, were inspiring.

I had a brief wobble when I was 11 when I discovered acting, through the school plays, and wanted to be an actor. But I soon realised I couldn't guarantee getting the best parts, so I gave that idea up. I've always had a somewhat pig-headed determination to be in charge of my own destiny.

B: I went to St Martin's School of Art (subsequently Central St Martins) in 1968, doing a Foundation Course then three years in Painting. The challenge I faced was being perceived as a 'nice middle class girl from the suburbs', destined to marry a tutor, care for him and have fashionable children. I certainly wasn't 'nice' and although I had a somewhat wild but productive time while I was at college, I secretly feared being tapped on the shoulder and told I couldn't be an artist, because I was a woman. There were barely any role models of women artists then, in reality or written about, so I felt lonely. The strategies that helped me

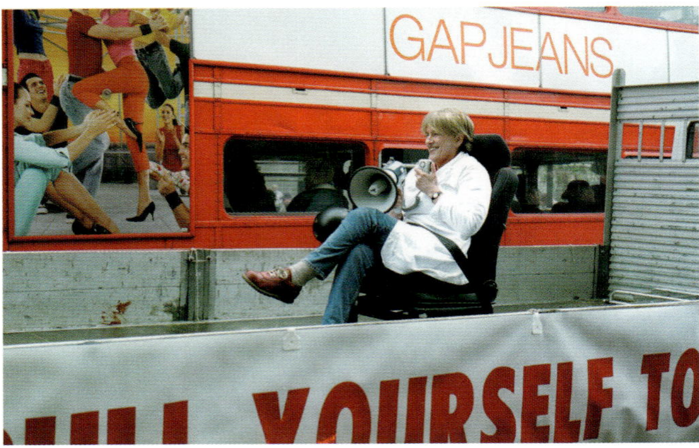

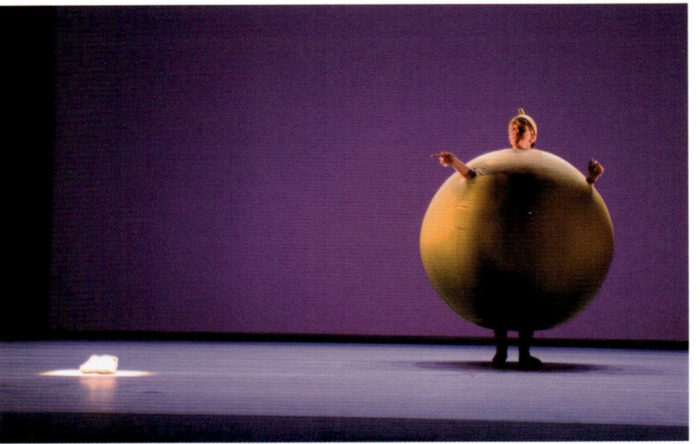

top left: *Pull Yourself Together,* performance, London, 2000. Commissioned by Live Art Development Agency/Adrian Heathfield/Tim Etchells as part of Small Acts for the Millennium. Photograph Hugo Glendenning

left: *How to Live*, performance, 2004. Part funded by a Wellcome Arts Award, and presented by Barbican, London. Photograph Andrew Whittuck

right: *Kitchen Show,* performance, 1991. Commissioned by London International Festival of Theatre. Photograph Andrew Whittuck

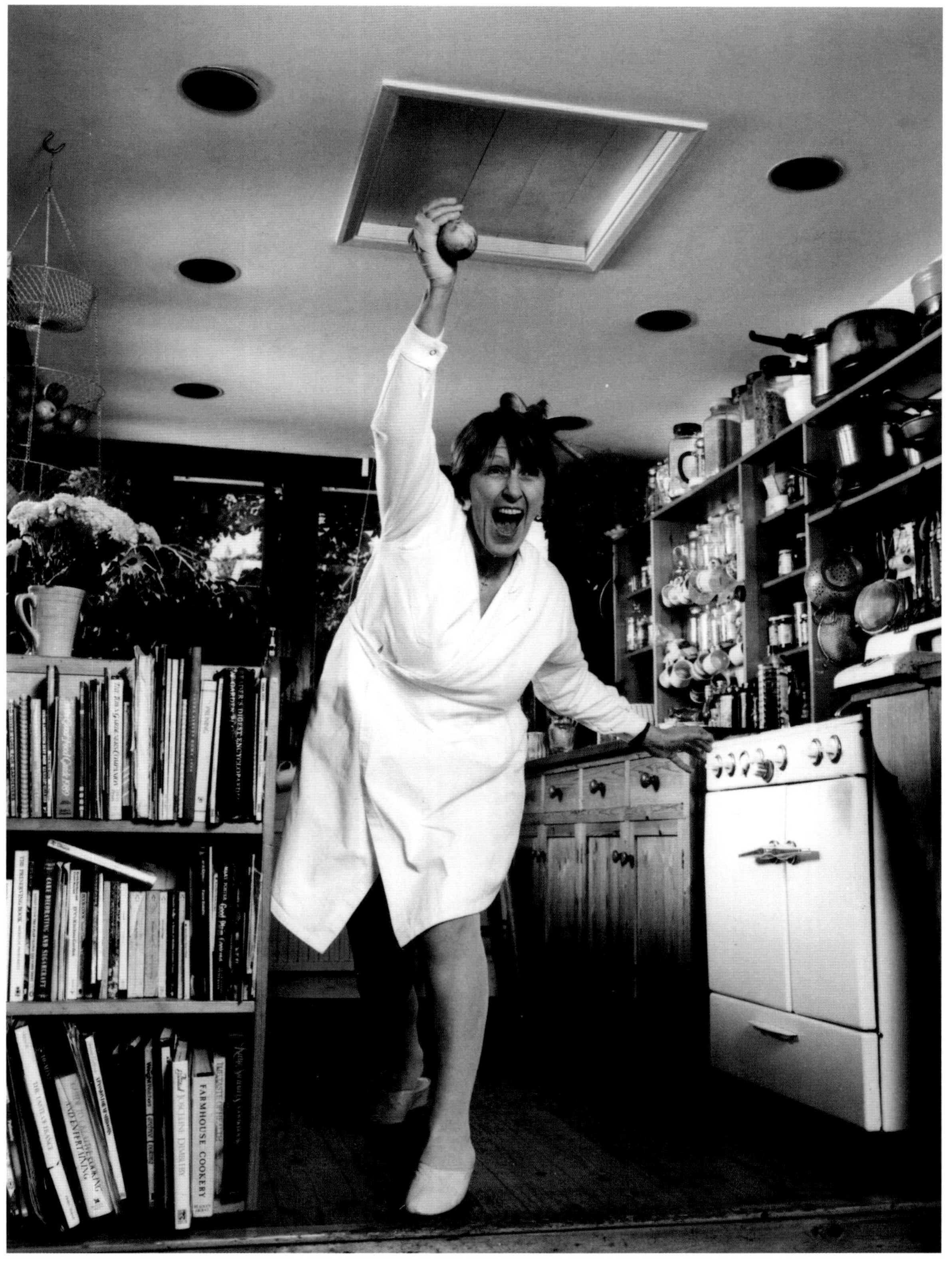
THE PRESERVING BOOK
CAKE DECORATING AND SUGARCRAFT
READER'S DIGEST ENCYCLOPAEDIA
THE TASTE OF FRANCE
AND ENTERTAINING
JOSCELINE DIMBLEBY
FARMHOUSE COOKERY

were my natural determination, and being a relentless, if somewhat naïve, optimist.

C: Although it's tempting to gnash one's teeth about the 'mainstream' art world, I find it rather a fruitless preoccupation. The powers that be for so long have been homogenous – male, white, middle class and so on. But that is changing, very slowly. My theory is that things adapt because mainstream art gets boring – and that great art, talent and brilliant ideas always win through. I've been on a quest to make art that tells new tales and reaches new audiences all my life, and that measures up as excellent. I don't succeed most of the time, but then, as I said, I'm an optimist.

D: I was fortunate to be an established artist before I 'came out' in 2000 as fitting the disability criteria defined by Arts Council England. The positive things that came out of this were meeting some great people and learning from them how to play that particular 'game'. Also there have been special funding opportunities like Unlimited for London 2012. Being part of the *Unlimited Festival* at Southbank Centre in 2012 was a marvelous experience.

But the downside is discovering what prejudice truly means and being seen as a 'risk', as 'other' despite an established track-record for reliability and quality of work. The bit I dislike most about it is what Clare Allen in her novel *Poppy Shakespeare* brilliantly describes as 'the harping league', where a hierarchy of suffering

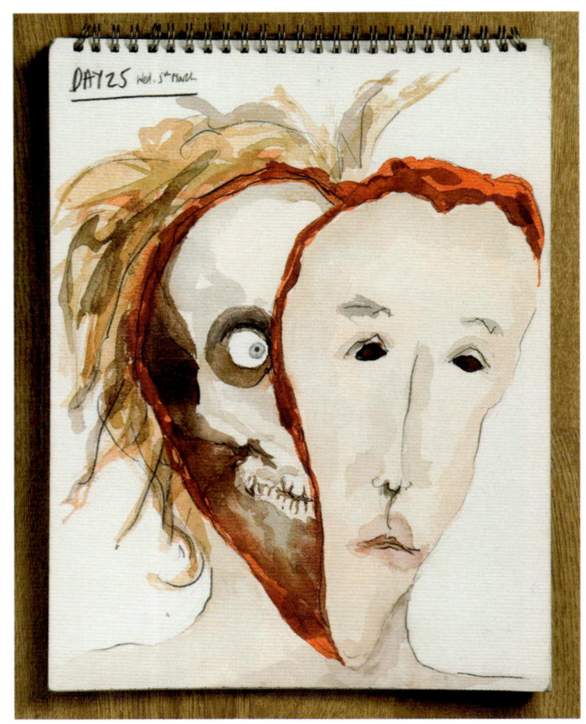

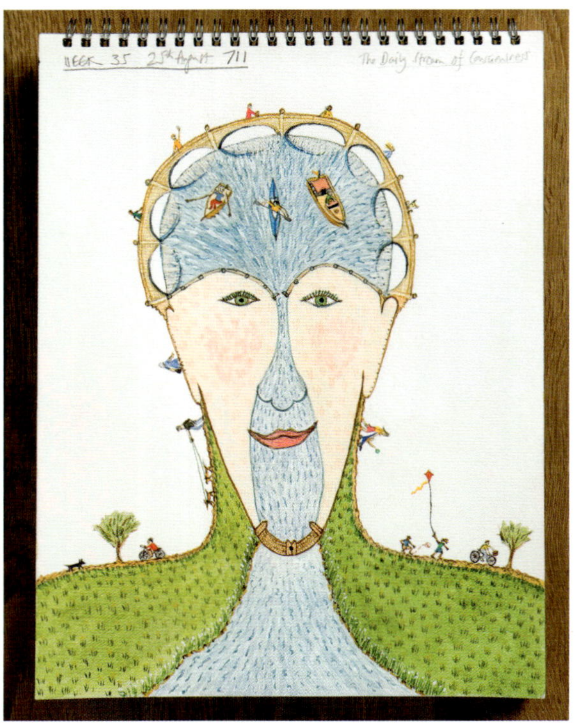

right: *Bobby Baker's Diary Drawings: Mental Illness and Me. 1997–2008. Day 25 & Day 711*, Watercolour, paper, 1997. Photograph Andrew Whittuck

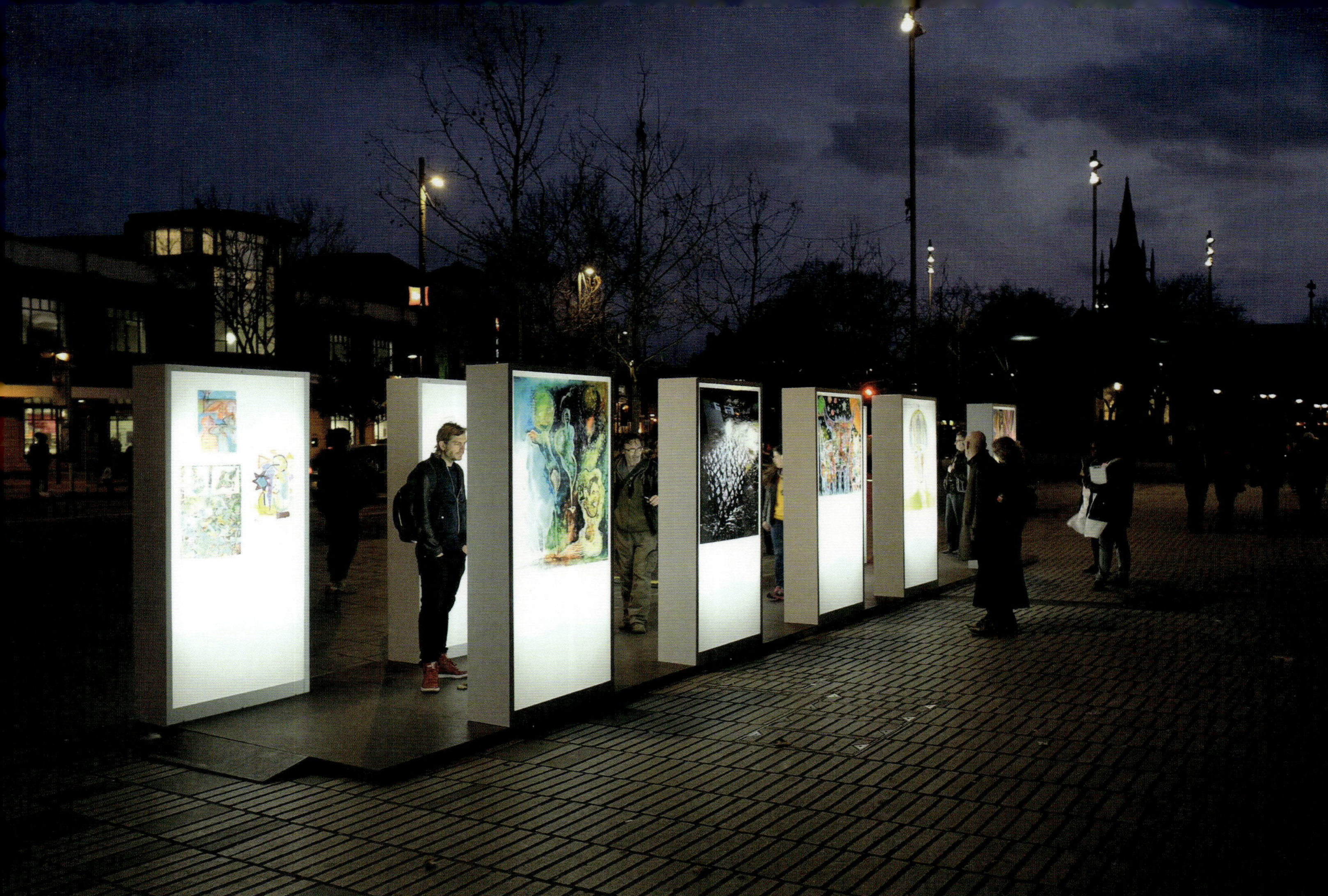

emerges. It's human nature to set these systems up, but it's dispiriting.

E: I'm a woman and an artist. That will do.

F: Here are two great quotes for those of us trying to do difficult things in challenging circumstances:

'Power can be taken, but not given. The process of the taking is empowerment in itself'. Gloria Steinham

'Success is not final, failure is not fatal: it is the courage to continue that counts'. Winston Churchill.

www.dailylifeltd.co.uk

above: *Letting in the Light,* lightbox installation, 2016. Stratford, London. Produced by Daily Life Ltd in partnership with Outside In and Bethlem Gallery, as part of Arts Council England Strategic Touring Programme. Photograph Andrew Whittuck

sean burn

A: mike crawford with the powis multi-arts project and pretty much by accident. just out ov hospital and newly housed, i went to to see if i could get a little typing time on their computer. mike invited us for a wee walk thru old aberdeen to test a donated camera with him. none ov the procedures he invited us to try made sense until i wz in the dark-room and watched that blank sheet ov paper form into black and white, an image i recognised as 'mine'. i wz smitten

B: career? strategies! please. its been a series ov accidents – happy and un. punctuated by illness/es. still is

C: well i do get told slightly less that *'oh we've already done madness'* or *'madness doesn't sell.'*

D: disability arts is an essential part ov diversity or rather diversities; which are all about reclaiming narrative/s; about taking control. we have been stifled, categorised, talked down to, ignored or otherwise denied for so long. our differences, here disabilities – in my case long-term mental distress – must be part ov the political, cultural, social narrative/s – and told from the inside too. my art tries to span categories, break down divides – but yes much is informed by mental distress (mine and others), and much ov which is explicitly disability art – art by those ov us with disabilities that talks about disability, raises debate, places it in public somehow. disability art has to be part ov the mainstream, belonging on the streets, in galleries, online, everywhere. now watch out for the coming mad studies insurrection!

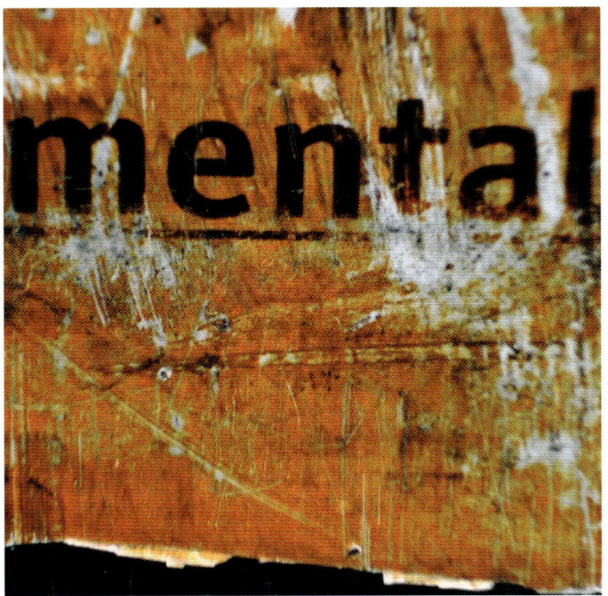

E: i am a writer, performer and outsider artist with active involvement in disability arts based on my own long-term lived experience ov mental distress. i'm part ov the north-east mad studies collective and promote cultural interventions around madness/es. my long-term goal is *'reclaiming the languages ov lunacy'.*

F: art is typically viewed as *'canon'* – a hierarchical pyramid in which some artists are great, the rest ov us are not. forget it! seriously.

left: *mental* (from staunch), photograph, 25 x 25cm, 2010
Photograph sean burn

right: *nutcase*, assemblage (nuts, marker pen, plastic container), from 20 x 11 x 4cm +, 2011. The New Art Gallery Walsall in association with DASH – Disability Arts residency.
Photograph sean burn

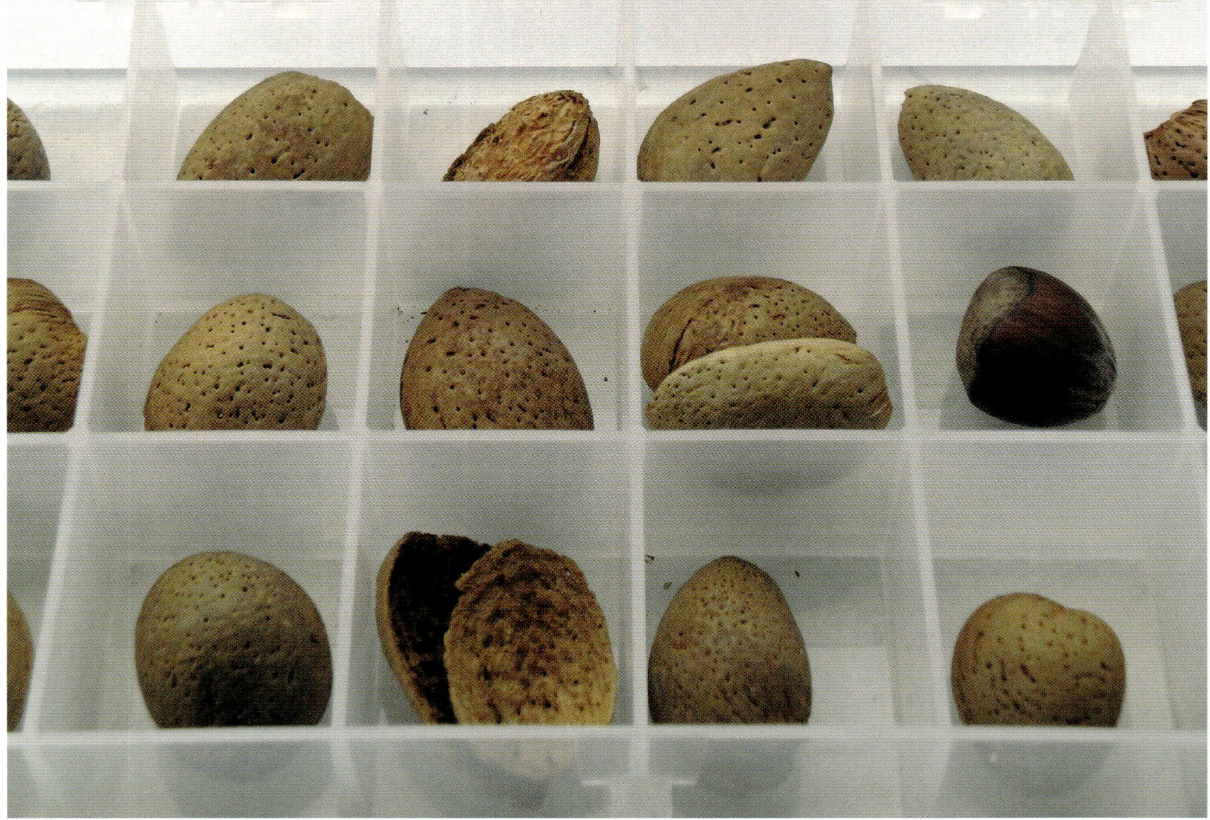
nutcase (a)
prototype
2010
s.b

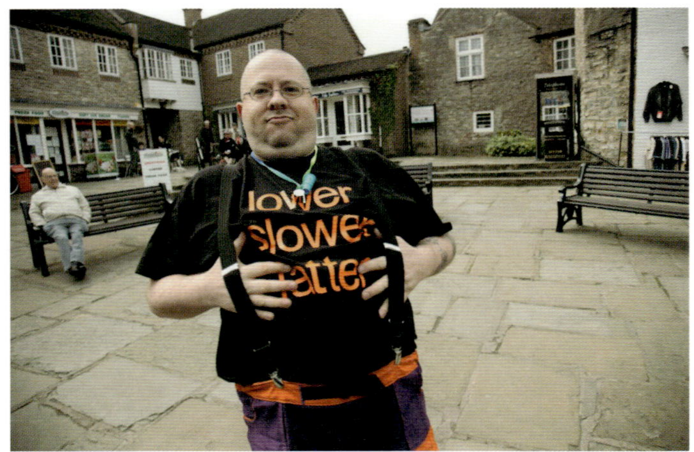

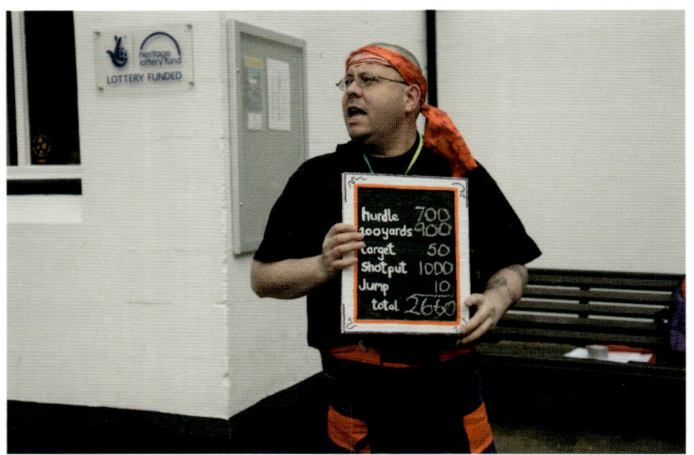

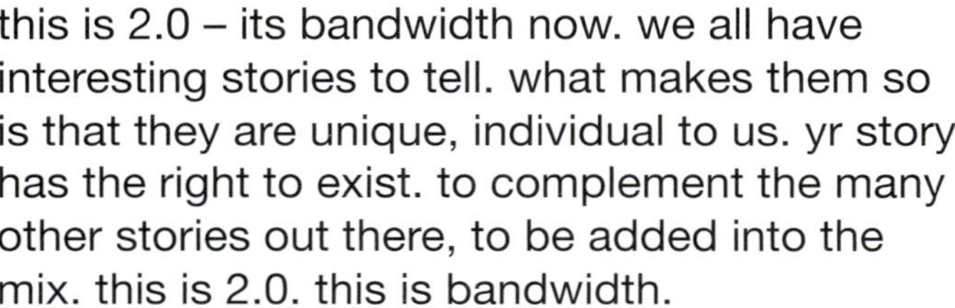

this is 2.0 – its bandwidth now. we all have interesting stories to tell. what makes them so is that they are unique, individual to us. yr story has the right to exist. to complement the many other stories out there, to be added into the mix. this is 2.0. this is bandwidth.

augusto boal talks ov the *'cop in the head'* – society, family (fami-lie?), patriarchy, education, religion, class, ableism/sanism, racism, heterosexuality etc which have all helped install it. the key trick ov control is that ultimately its a kind-ov self-inflicted panopticon and is hugely damaging – stifling, denying voice – particularly to those ov us who are different. so please dont give yrself a hard time, experiment, play, grow – discover touchstones and allies – those with similar (not the same) voices, those who inspire. above all give yrself permission to do all this

www.gobscure.info
http://madstudiesne.weebly.com/

above: *psychosis belly*, live art, duration variable, summer 2012. M21 Unlimited funded Disability Arts festival, Much Wenlock, Shropshire created by DASH and Live Art Development Agency. Photograph Richard Foot

right: *those ov us who have learnt to love our madnesses,* digital art printed onto tee-shirts, 2011. The New Art Gallery Walsall in association with DASH – Disability Arts residency. Photograph sean burn

those ov us
who have learnt
to love our
madnesses

Juan delGado

A: At the age of thirteen when I was given a small portable film camera, I felt a growing inspiration inside to photograph those immediate objects that surrounded me. I also spent hours on my own arranging and piling up discarded objects that I had found in the street and began to experiment with light and shadows using a desktop lamp and a bath towel as a reflector.

Then I photographed them from every imaginable angle. It was an exciting time to learn, with the only advice I found in books.

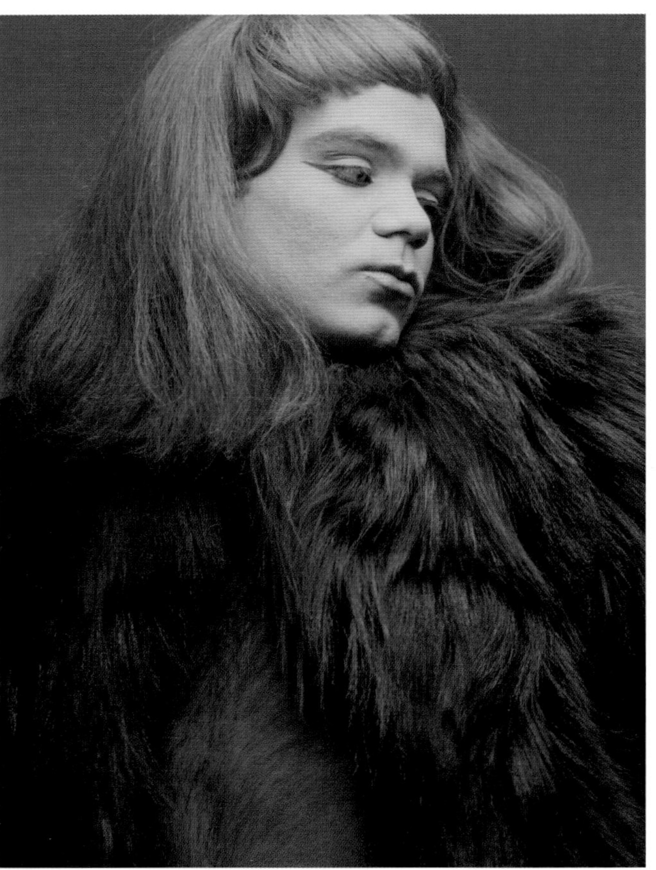

Every month I ran to the local kiosk to purchase the photo magazine; there I read the stories from the masters: Henri Cartier-Bresson, Yousef Koudelka, Lee Friedlander, Ansel Adams… As a young photographer, I was very interested in gender and sexuality, and found the work of Diane Arbus, Robert Mapplethorpe, Claude Cahun and Cindy Sherman extraordinarily inspiring.

B: Art was not considered a profession in Spain, more like an entertainment for the high classes; I chose to study photography, but there was a lack of opportunities to progress and develop professionally. I worked hard to get my first camera, a 35mm Olympus and later, I managed to have my own photolab where I could process and experiment with film and other materials. I had my first exhibitions in local pubs and the community centre.

Despite the difficulties, I was determined to succeed and finally I found a job as a press photographer. However, due to my hearing loss, I faced tremendous difficulties in dealing with clients; also it was very challenging to meet people at social events. In 1994, I decided to move to London and joined a course in Portraiture and Architectural Photography. I enrolled in the University of Westminster and graduated with a distinction for my degree in Contemporary Media Practice

left: *Diafragma* (Series *Transformers*), photograph, 100 x 80cm, 1996. London, UK. Photograph Juan delGado

right: *Sediments,* on-site Installation, 50 x 76cm, 2008. Vivid Media/Culture Lab. Photograph Juan delGado

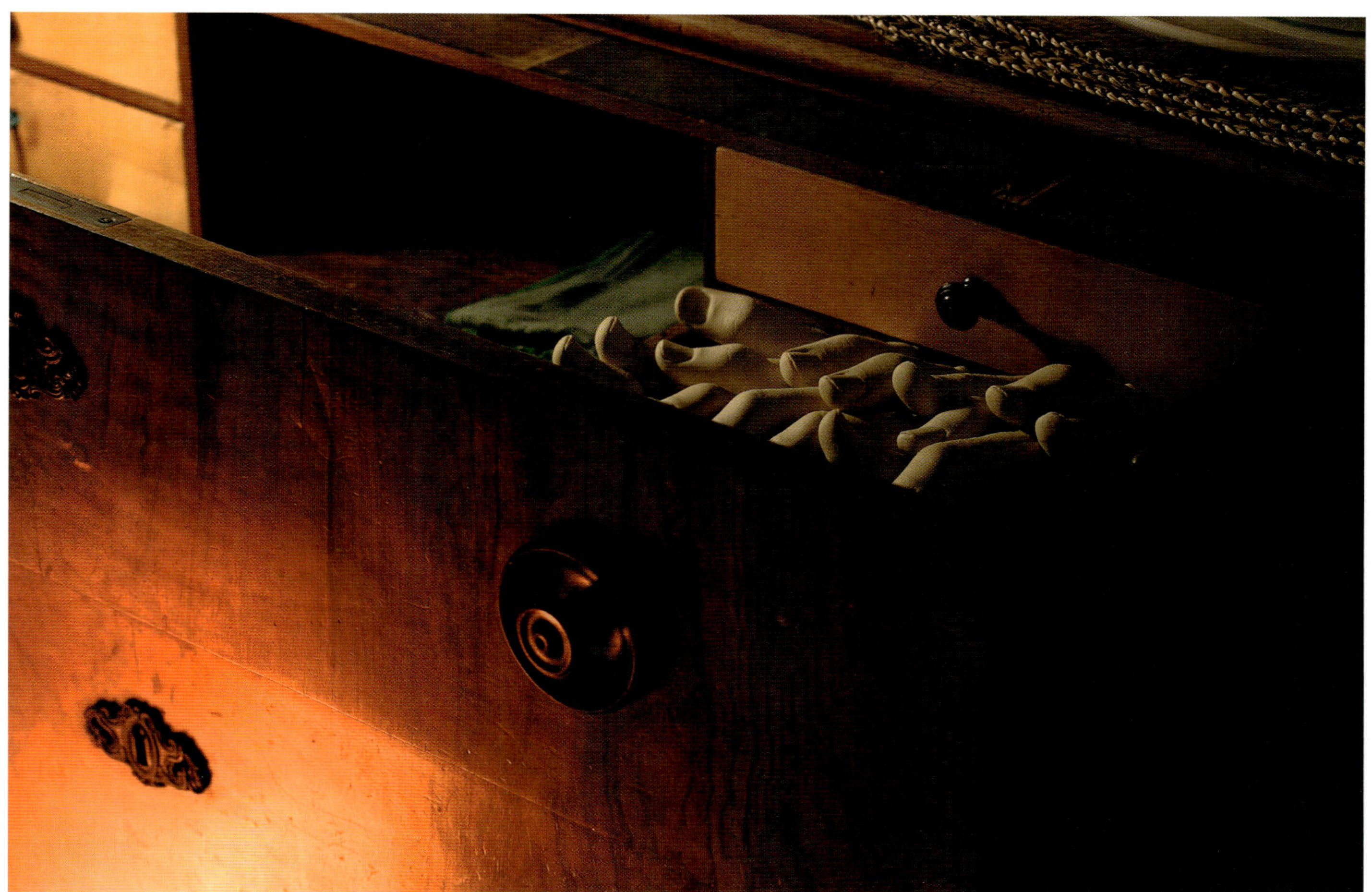

for my dissertation 'Trans-sexuality in the Spanish Cinema 1971–1999'.

C: At that time, I entered into contact with the London Disability Arts Forum, an amazing platform ran by Çağlar Kimyoncu, Julie McNamara and Chas de Swiet. They also published a monthly magazine called DAiL whose main editor was Joe McConnell. This period put in me touch with other artists who identified themselves as Disabled. I was very inspired by artists such as Bobby Baker, Yinka Shonibare and Nancy Willis. Participating in the Disability Film Festival that was organized with the support of many enthusiastic volunteers, gave me the motivation to continue my training.

I progressed into a MA in Media Practice that I completed with the production of my first video installation called *'Don't Look Under the Bed'*. It was September 2001 when I presented my first moving image work at the Lux Cinema. My photography series *'The Wounded Image'* was also selected for the John Kobal Photographic Portrait Award and exhibited at the National Portrait Gallery in London and National Gallery in Edinburgh.

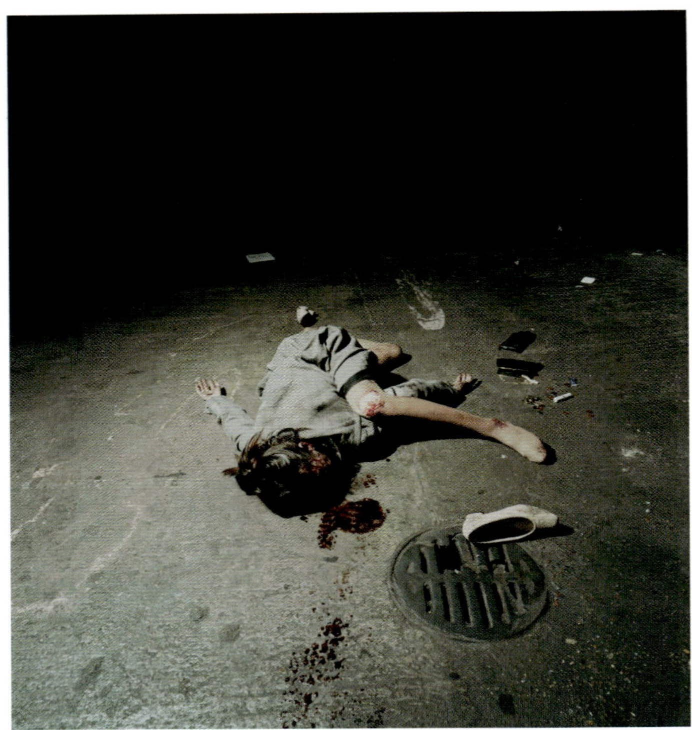

Untitled #12 (Series *The Wounded Image*), photograph, 100 x 100cm, 2002. London, UK. Photograph Juan delGado

I have always combined my studies with the production of art, mainly photography and later moving image and installation. In 1995, I was selected to exhibit at the Royal Festival Hall and to present my work in the Conference *'The Way We Live Now'* about gender and sexuality. I also tried to develop relationships with private galleries and due to the nature of my work, which was labeled as 'difficult' to sell, I directed my efforts to work with public institutions both in the UK and Internationally. I was lucky to receive support from Wellcome Trust, Arts Council England, and the Jerwood Space.

D: The London Disability Film Festival in all its editions represented a turning point in the way moving image works, including documentaries and video art became more accessible to diverse audiences. The increasingly available digital and portable technologies allowed independent filmmakers and video artists to produce work that finally have an audience. I was lucky to present two of my works, *'The Passion of Theresa'* and *'Don't Look Under the Bed'* at the National Film Theatre and later at the Vee – TV series, Channel 4.

Also the role led by *Shape* to support Deaf and Disabled artists was crucial to bring confidence to many who were still confined to invisibility from the mainstream arts. In collaboration with other organizations, such as *Artsadmin*, which were developing schemes to support Disabled and Deaf artists through bursaries for research and development, artists' advice sessions and specific training workshops on professional development, they offered invaluable assistance to my career. Other organisations such as *Dada-South* and the courageous work of its director Stevie Rice was essential to becoming more confident in my practice.

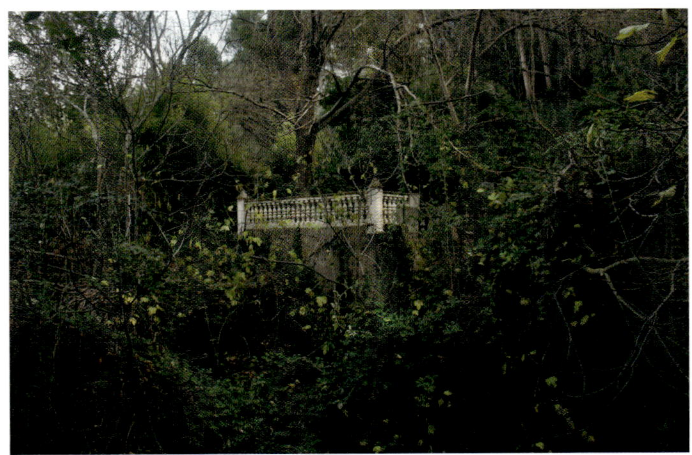

Balcony (Series *Altered Landscapes*), photograph, 50 x 76cm, 2011. London. Photograph Juan delGado

Finally, having the opportunity to be awarded an *Unlimited* commission in 2014 greatly helped me to become more visible, to bring my work to an international audience. I also invested a great amount of time and energy to make my work accessible, encouraging venues where I exhibited to explore ways to make exhibitions accessible.

E: When it comes to identity I always remember Stuart Hall when he mentioned that identity is closely connected to our experience as living beings. Life brings to us new experiences every moment, every day… so our identity is evolving every moment.

He said the more attached we become to our identity the less open we are to that which life offers to us. Every moment is the present and every experience gives me the opportunity to discover many things about myself and also about others. I am a curious person, a traveller, and I consider life a journey to learn from others. To me, the 'other' is the fountain in which I answer my desire for knowledge. It is through this encounter with the unknown that I will learn things that were dormant, waiting to manifest themselves.

F: Everyone of us has a tremendous potential; we just have to unleash our drive to express the unique way we experience the world.

Since 2013, I have been producing *'Qisetna : Talking Syria'*, an online platform which aims to collect stories from Syrians who are displaced inside their country or living in exile. During these years, I have encountered many young people, whose reply to my request to collect their story would ask, *'but Juan, who is interested in my story?'*

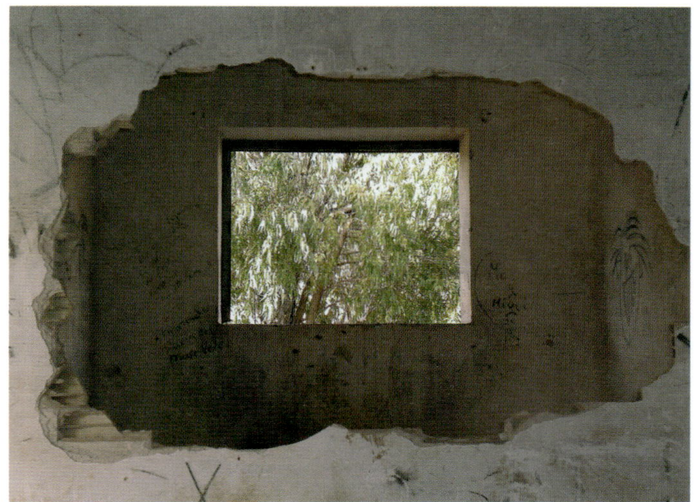

Untitled #2 (Series *Windows*), photograph, 35 x 45cm, 2010. Valencia, Spain. Photograph Juan delGado

I would say: *'I am; I am interested in your story. And I think many people will be extremely surprised to read the story of a young Syrian talking about her or his dreams; how was life back in Syria before the war… we will be amazed to learn you are a human being as we'.*

These young people will then dig into their personal history, the traumatic experience they are going through, and yet they will write a story for me to share in my blog. Because now they know for certain that somebody cares for them.

www.juandelgado.co
www.talkingsyria.com

Rachel Gadsden

A: I grew up in the Middle East and didn't visit an art gallery until I was 18 years of age – but I have always had a vivid visual imagination and throughout my childhood I was forever drawing and painting. Ultimately, somehow instinctively, it seemed to be my destination to be an artist.

B: The artistic world is very competitive and although I am not proud of the fact I did this now, I spent a huge amount of energy hiding my disability as much as possible at commission interviews and in front of selection panels. I was fearful that my disabilities would be an additional barrier for commissioners to consider, and I have no doubt it was.

Ultimately, my artistic career began to emerge and significant commissions and residencies happened and I no longer felt I needed to hide anything, as my work spoke for itself. Additionally, there was beginning to be a cultural shift in perceptions of disability, not a huge shift, but a shift none-the-less. The relief to be able to present exactly who I am as an individual was huge, my work is inspired by my

below: *I Found You,* mixed media on velvet, 230 x 180cm (triptych), 2012. Unlimited – London 2012 Cultural Olympiad (Arts Council England & British Council UK & South Africa) Created as part of Unlimited Global Alchemy Exhibition 2012. Photograph Rachel Gadsden

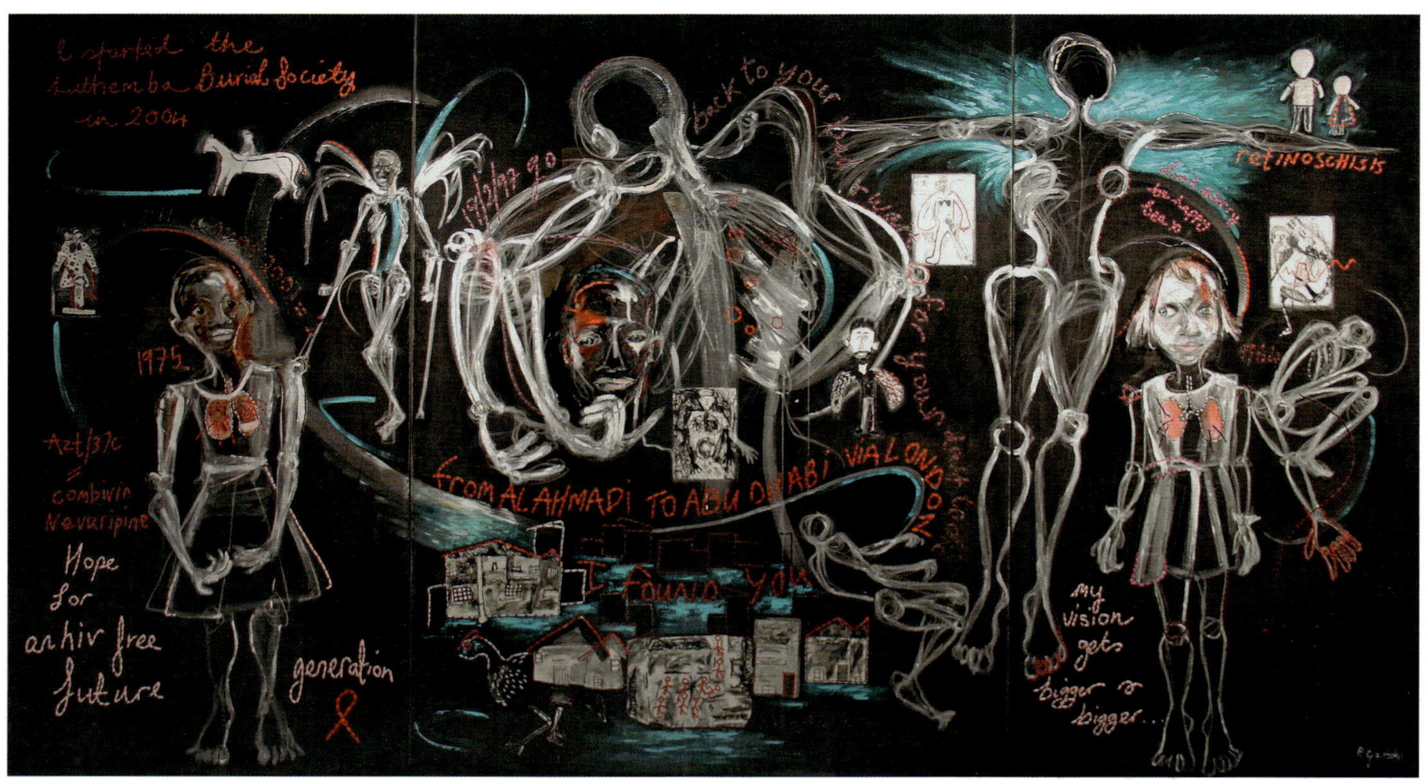

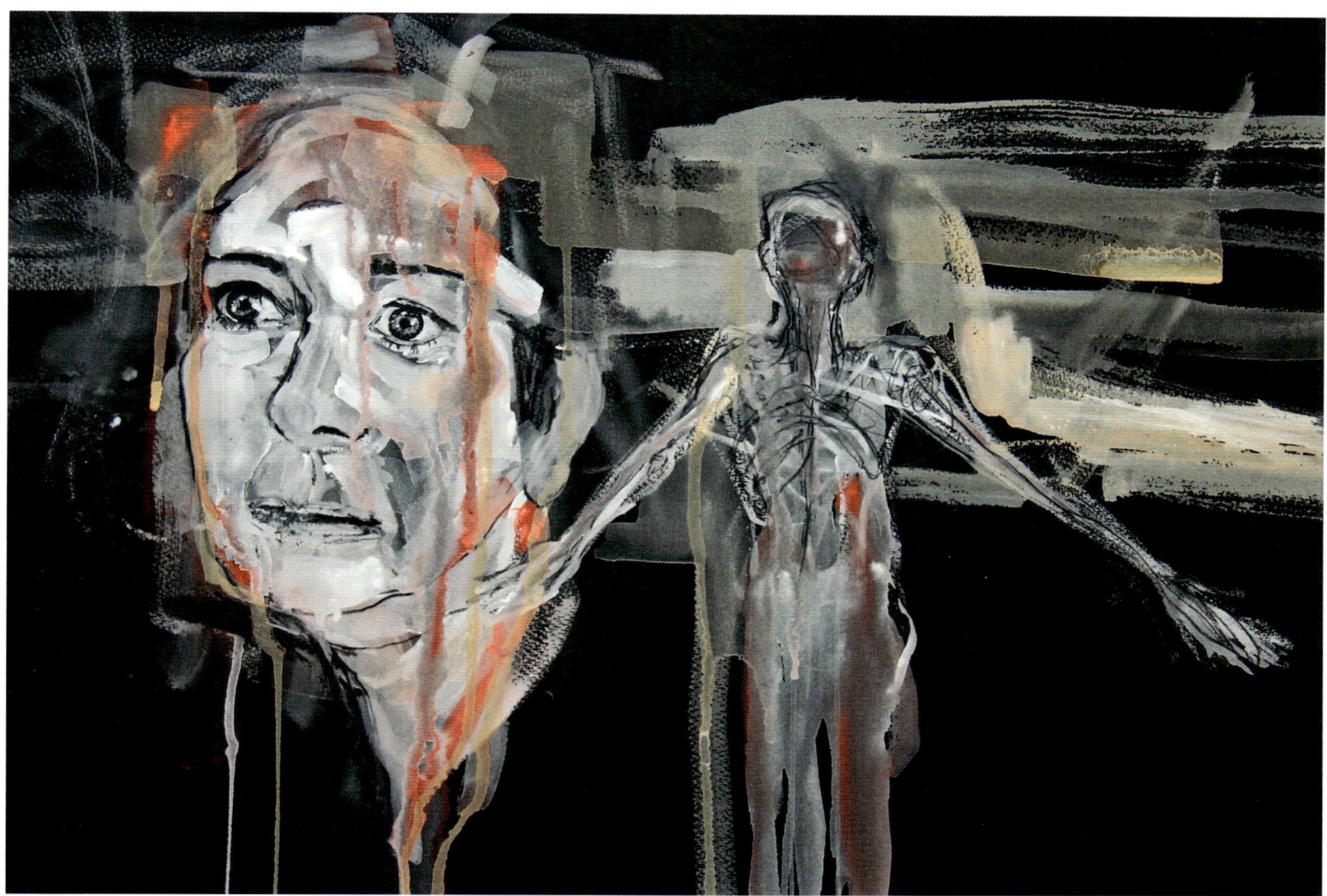

human experience and being disabled is all part of that notion.

C: In 2008 I was appointed the first contemporary artist-in-residence at Hampton Court Palace since Holbein's time and undertook a year long residency culminating in a major solo exhibition. Throughout my career I have undertaken as many projects and commissions with so called *'mainstream'* museums and within the mainstream art worlds as I have with disability organisations and festivals etc. I make work that considers universal notions of the human condition – beyond any considered differences, whether they are to do with sexuality, ethnicity or disability. We are ultimately all human and I explore this issue – maybe that is a factor as to why my work sits within a disability as well as a mainstream context – this is a tricky thing to quantify!

D: The existence of the Disability Art movement is incredibly empowering – I was born with my

above: *Precious,* mixed media on paper, 89 x 108cm, 2015. Photograph Rachel Gadsden

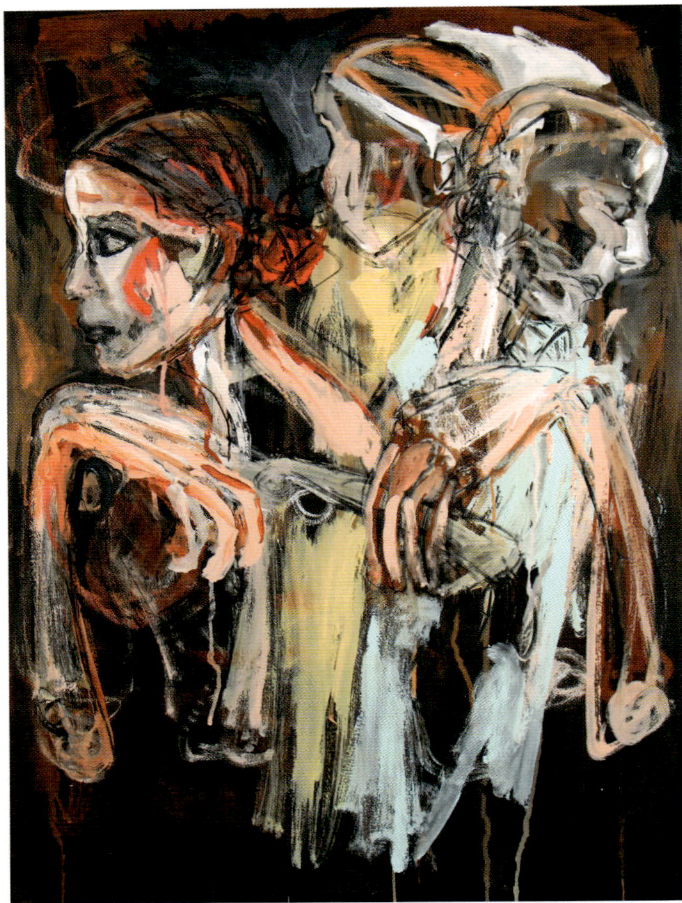

Trace of Memory III, mixed media on paper, 95 x 76cm, 2013. Photograph Rachel Gadsden

disabilities and they massively impact on my daily experience, and part of my work is about active activism. As someone who has overcome some of the barriers that affect Disabled people, I use my artistic vision and presence to build collaborative artistic projects, that seek to give vulnerable individuals throughout the Globe a creative voice to be able to fight stigma and to bring further cultural change to their communities. Ultimately the Disability Art movement has done a huge amount to change perceptions of disability and I feel very proud to be part of the movement.

E: I am Disabled and severely visually impaired and I now always define myself in this way – I have a responsibility to do this, and through my voice as a Disabled artist I believe I should be a role model for younger emerging artists and I take this responsibility very seriously. I only wish there had been Disabled artists to support me at the early stages of my career, and if there had been, I absolutely know I would never have felt the need to hide my disabilities at the early stages of my career, as I regrettably did.

F: Work as hard as you can and develop the strongest artistic and contextual skills that you can so that your work is as powerful as possible. Also make sure you get your work out into the public domain whenever you can. Live, breathe, and embrace your artistic vision 24 hours a day – luck has nothing to do with being successful as many successful artists will tell you! You need to have bucket loads of courage that is for sure, but ultimately the rewards will emerge.

www.rachelgadsden.com
vimeo.com/rachelgadsden

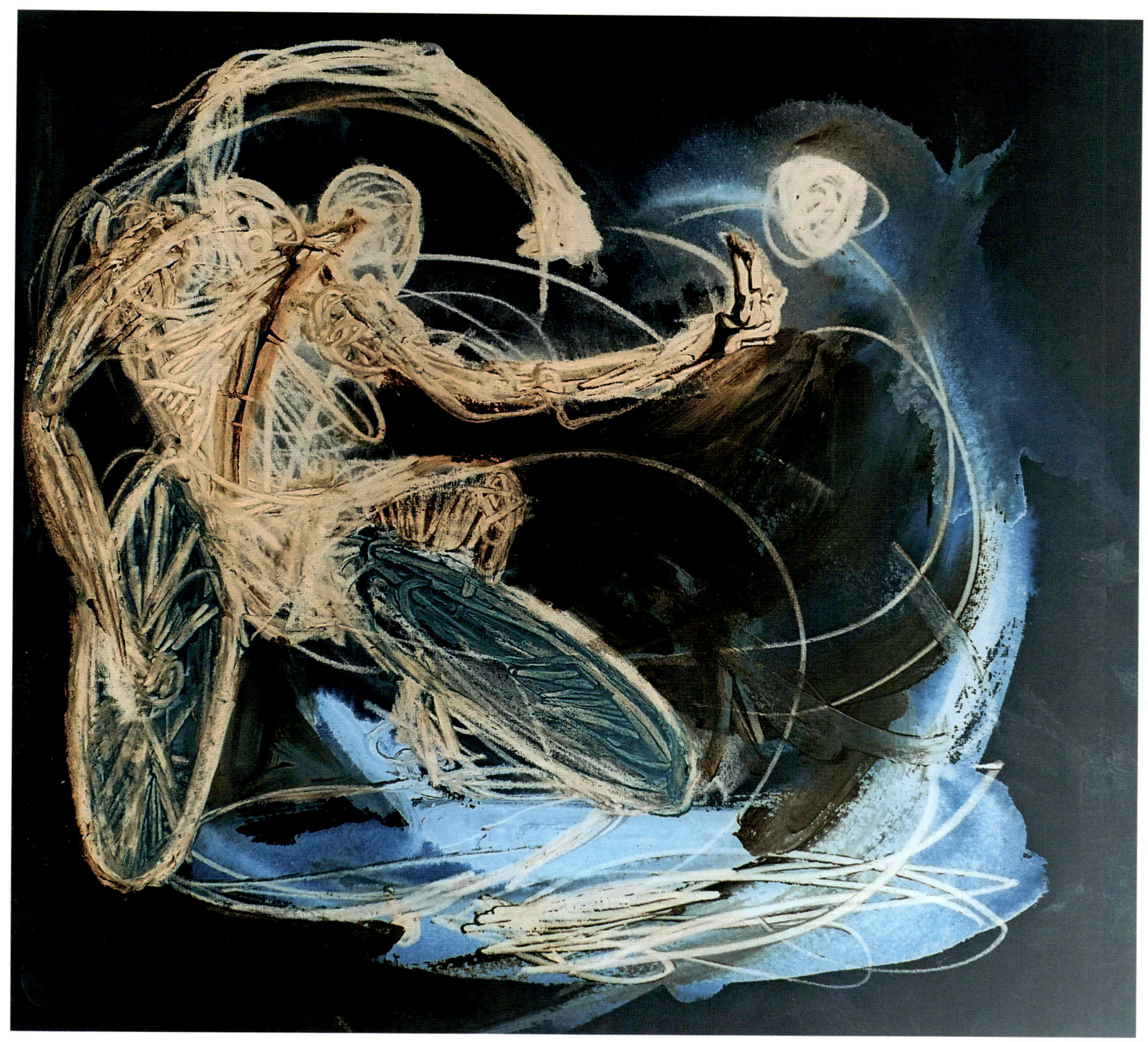

Power, mixed media on paper, 30 x 25cm, 2016. Photograph Rachel Gadsden

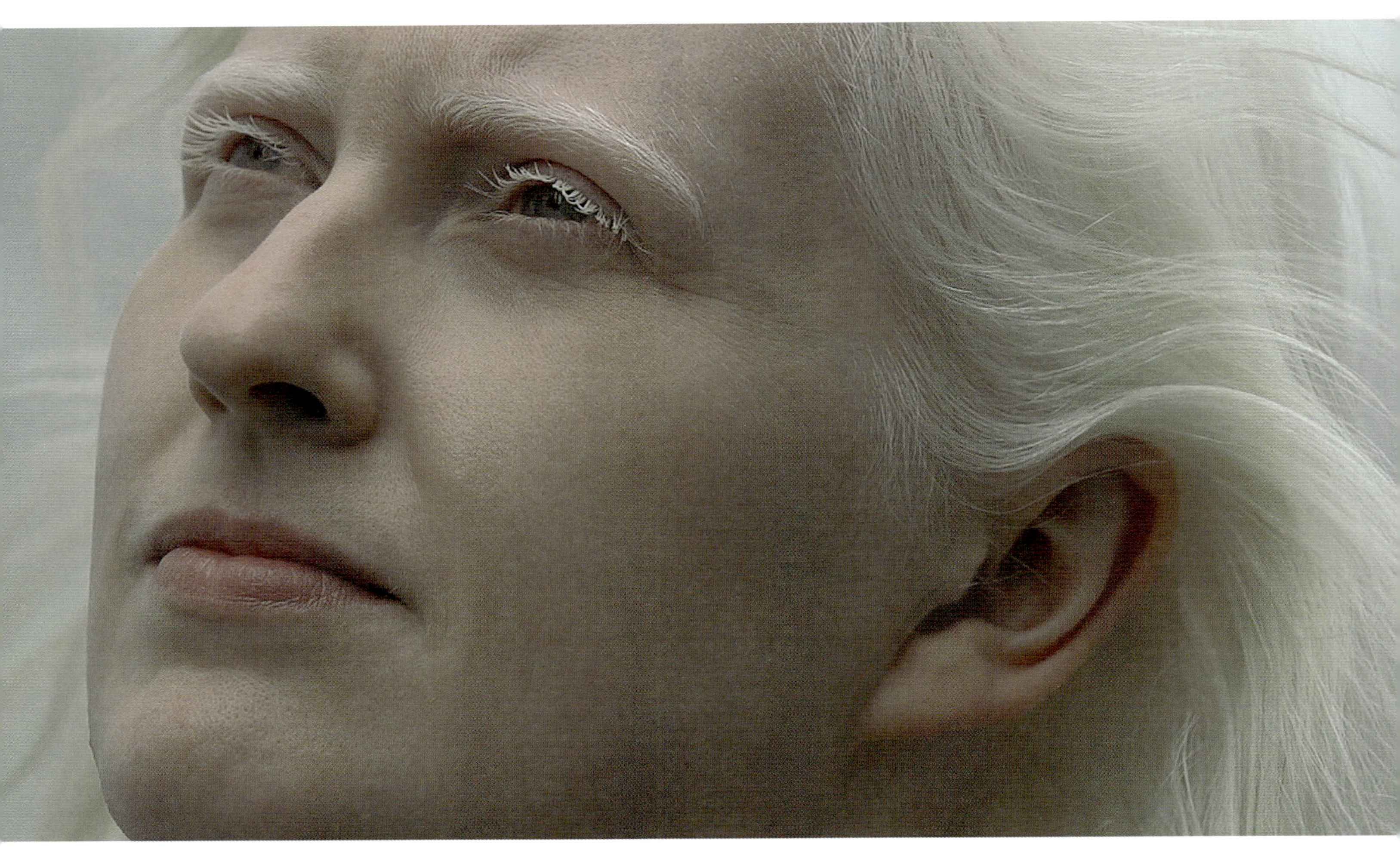

David Hevey

A: I was a young, alienated, under-class, 6th of 7 children, from an Irish immigrant family, living in a council estate. I was proper alienated working class. Just when it couldn't get any more weird, it did: I got epilepsy. This was both the final, terrible end, and the enlightening beginning of the rest of my life. It was the final terrible end because I assumed that *'it'* would send me mad or kill me in some way. And the only positive, oddly, was that the same visions I got in epilepsy, somehow released comparable visual ability in art. So, the only choice left, was Art.

B: As with the first answer, solutions live very close to problems. The problems I faced were enormous, but I didn't know it. I got into Art School by copying the guy next to me's list of O Levels, and when I was in, I worked like I had worked in the factory: I started early, I finished late, and I worked on Saturdays. Then when I graduated, I presumed, being working class that I was a bit thick and everyone else was a bit clever, so I better keep learning. I came from so far down, I didn't know where etiquette, correct behavior, how to hustle the players, etc. were. So I got on with what I thought was right aesthetically, which was trying to make art to change the world.

C: I work in the mainstream and on the margins. I often say my work is about diverse perspectives on the mainstream, because, actually, that is what the mainstream really is: a collection or conflation of once divergent forces. Wagner was on the margins once! I create work for most of the UK (and much international) cultural landscape, from the BBC to the Arts Council and so on, and those mainstreams need, like oxygen, the original voices, stories and art of the outsider, told from the margins about the mainstream: basically, all powerful work is, somewhere, about that the way we live now, mainstream or margins.

D: For me, meeting the Disability Rights/Arts Movement was a huge revelation and a life-changer. I came out about epilepsy but, unlike many other people with impairments, that also

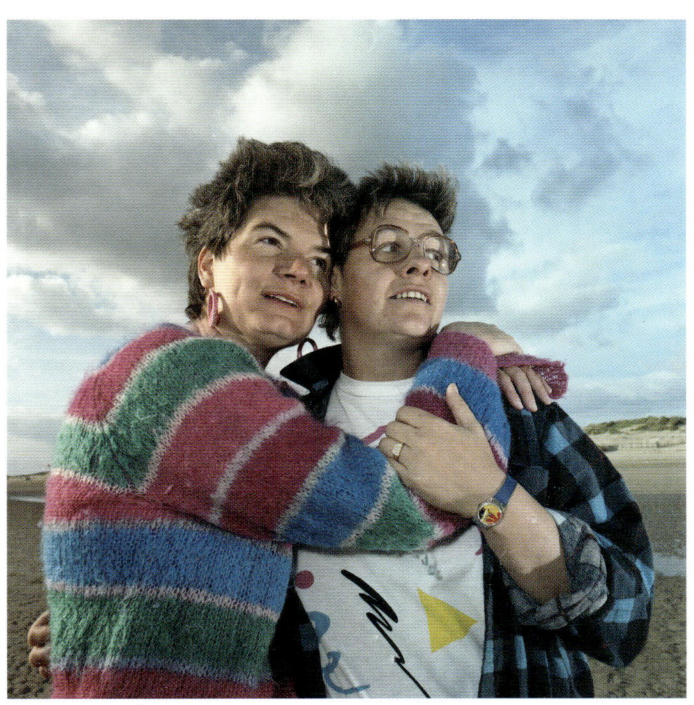

left: Unlimited/Jo Bannon production still, photograph, 2015. Unlimited, Shape Arts, Arts Admin, et al. Photograph David Hevey

right: *Clair and Geraldine In Love Again*, photograph, 1992. Camerawork. Photograph David Hevey

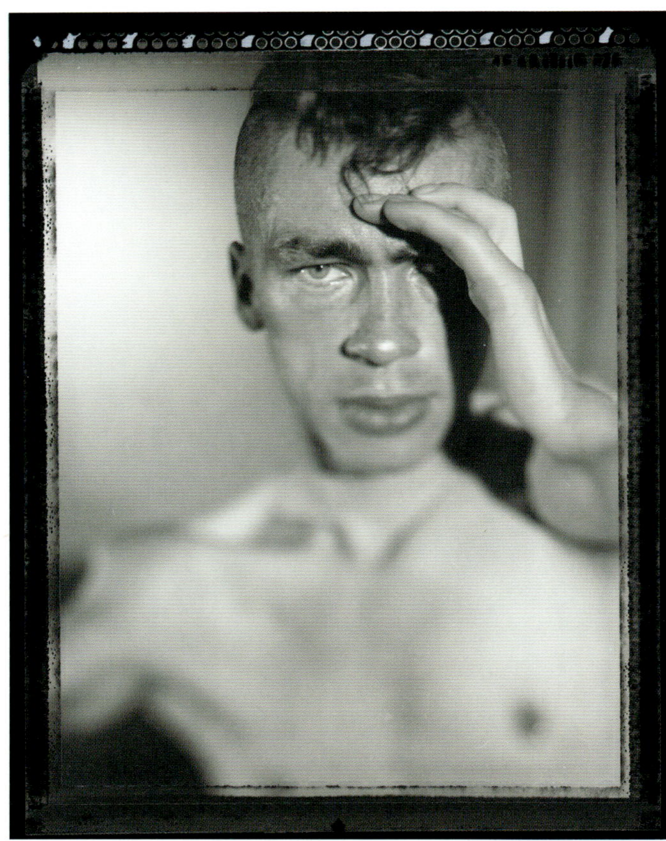

began a twin-track of a journey out of having epilepsy. So, it changed my life in more ways than one. I also felt, back in the day, that the way outsiders were portrayed was wrong – and set out to do something about it, which led me to writing *Creatures* for Routledge, on to making *The Disabled Century* for the BBC, and so on.

So, it was in my life: I don't think it has hindered my career, it has been one part of my career and has been good for those who fought for rights, and made great culture about those fights which gave birth to the Disability Arts movement. But so has aiming high, making big events work to audiences in the millions.

above: *The Disabled Century* production still, photograph 1999/2012. BBC. Photograph David Hevey

right: *Freak Out* production still, photograph, 1995. BBC. Photograph David Hevey

E: I call myself a media professional, making work about the way we live now. In fact, I never really talk about myself because I am not in the brief! I get commissioned to make work about others' lives, to get deep under the skin of the way people live now, and create film, media and art based on the championing of those lives. I get described by others quite often, and I don't ever contest or argue with others' definitions. I don't think I was borne out of the Disability Arts movement, but I have a huge respect for it: I like counter-culture, I like the voices of those who fought hegemony, but I like, also, to work across many margins and cultures, delivering all kinds of stories for clients.

F: Be radical. Everything's a dying order, help the old world die. And all clients, really, want to change the world. Do research. All the funding organisations are in constant flux and need to find the *'new'*. Find what you care about, and try to make work for those things, which should include railing against the existing order. Above all, name the barriers and attack them. Find out a) how you want to change the world, and join it with b) how organisations want to change the world, and c) pitch your story to those areas. Above all, drive fear, too, into the clients – make them fear you just might lean across the table and kick off if they say no to your vision!

www.davidhevey.com

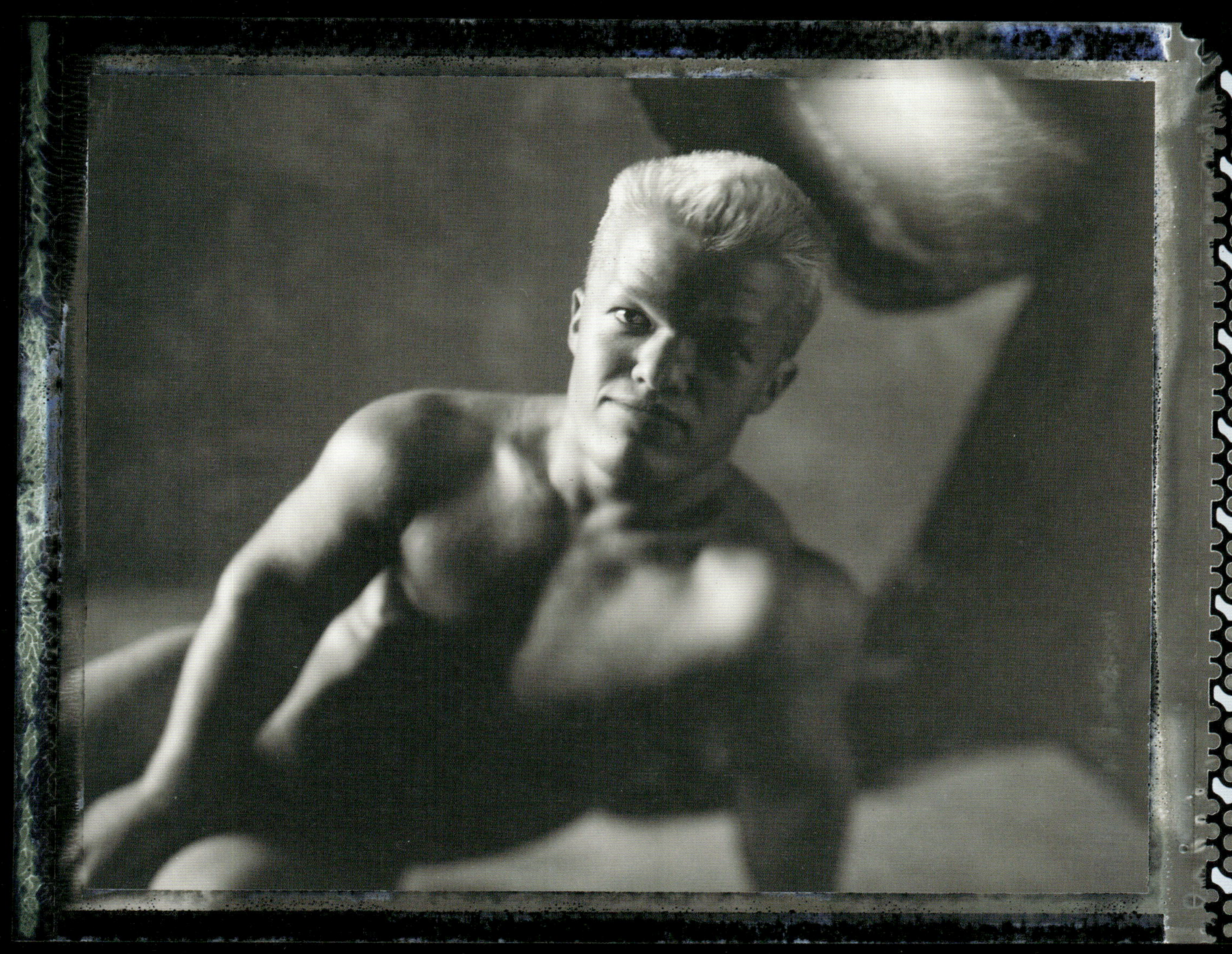

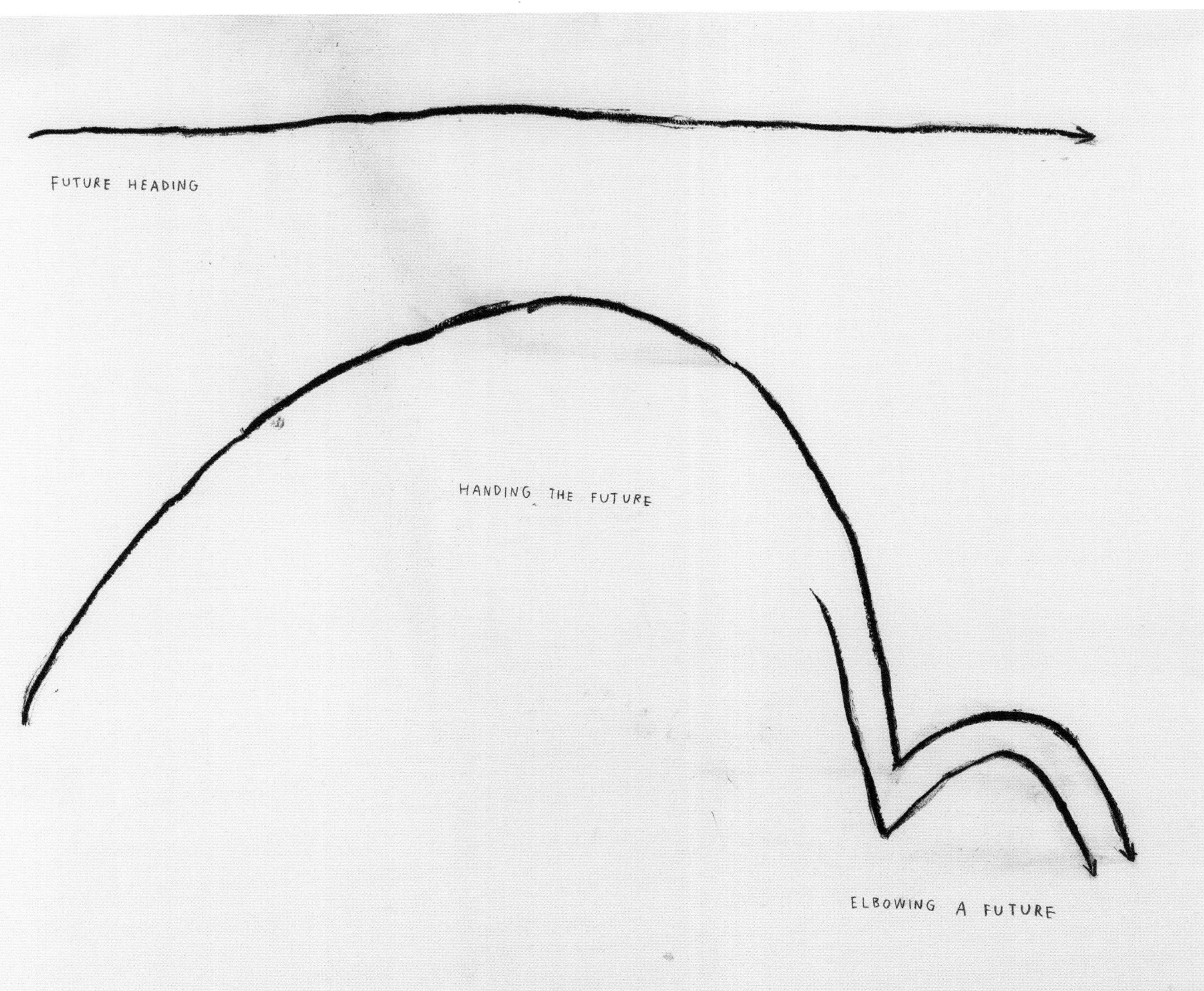
FUTURE HEADING
HANDING THE FUTURE
ELBOWING A FUTURE

Christine Sun Kim

A: When young, I would spend so much time on colouring books and would marvel at how colours can go beyond colours like scent and time. But the reason for being an artist continues to evolve as I get older. As an adult, I love it that there's no routine in being an artist; my schedule and work pace vary on a daily basis.

B: I didn't fully grasp on what it takes to be an artist and I didn't have mentors or financial support. I got really lucky with my full time job, because my boss often granted me schedule flexibility to do residencies and attend graduate school. I stubbornly kept on applying for a number of grants and residencies for years and things started to come together, mainly because my art started to mature over the time. I often work with non-signers, so being equipped with social and collaborative skills came to be the biggest tool I've ever had.

C: There are plenty of assholes out there, so use your difference to filter them out fast and don't spend too much time with them. I've found a group of solid/real people to work with and have been with them for years. Sometimes I like to venture into non-art worlds, so I wouldn't feel suffocated and I've always been in-between and I thrive on that, I think.

left: *Elbowing a Future,* dry pastel and pencil on paper, 100 x 125cm, June 2015. Photograph Christine Sun Kim

top right: *TBD TBC TBA,* charcoal on paper, 28 x 38cm January 2015. Photograph Christine Sun Kim

right: *Too Possessive For Score,* charcoal on paper, 28 x 38cm, January 2015. Photograph Christine Sun Kim

D: ***[It]*** *(The 'Disability Arts movement)* has greatly helped, especially in America and the UK, because there seems to be a lot of financial support coming from that angle. I could easily ask for sign language interpreters without feeling anxious and worrying about being a burden to organisers, and I would say to myself 'So is this

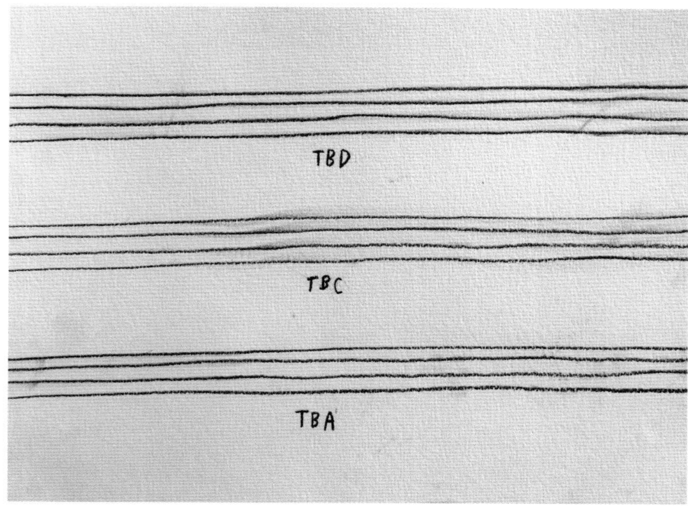

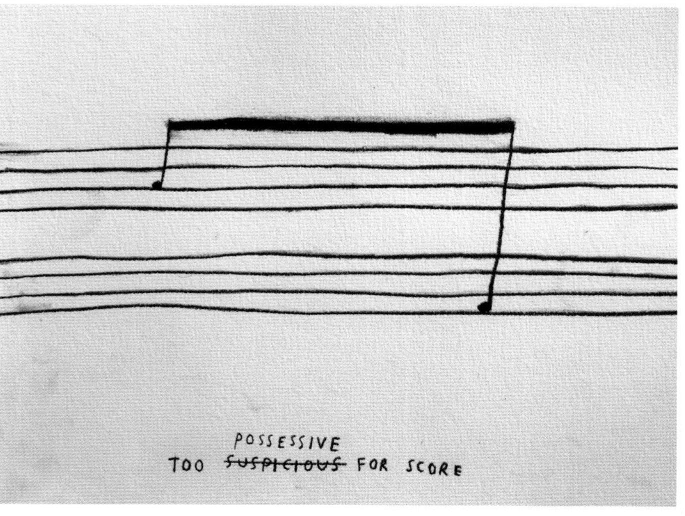

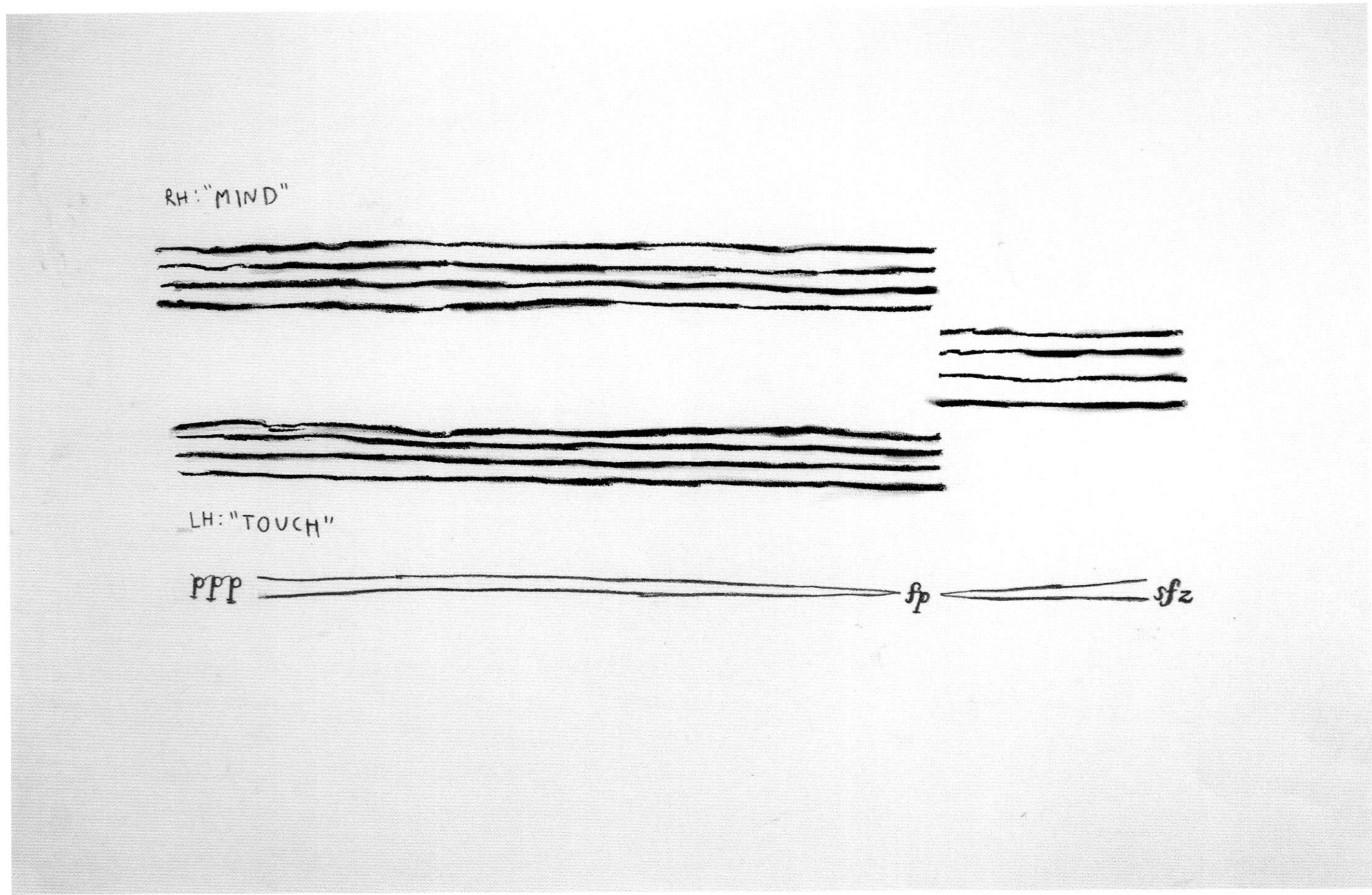

how artists feel? I want that all the time.' It's a nice reminder. However, I'm not comfortable being called a Disabled artist nor artist with a disability. I feel that the term 'disability' still holds an amount of stigma that I want to avoid. I hope this movement will continue over the time until 'disability' is fully reclaimed by us.

E: I am an artist. I wouldn't want to be called a female artist all the time, nor Korean-American artist, nor Deaf artist. I want my work to be recognised as work alone, without too much of my identity in context. But, due to many reasons such as the press, people deem it necessary to mention my difference. It's like acknowledging a white elephant in the room before they can move onto my art... and I get it.

F: It's easy to get angry and don't let that pull you down. Use anger as your fuel and be with people who truly believe in your work.

christinesunkim.com

above: *Mind Touch,* dry pastel and pencil on paper, 55 x 75cm, January 2016. Photograph Christine Sun Kim

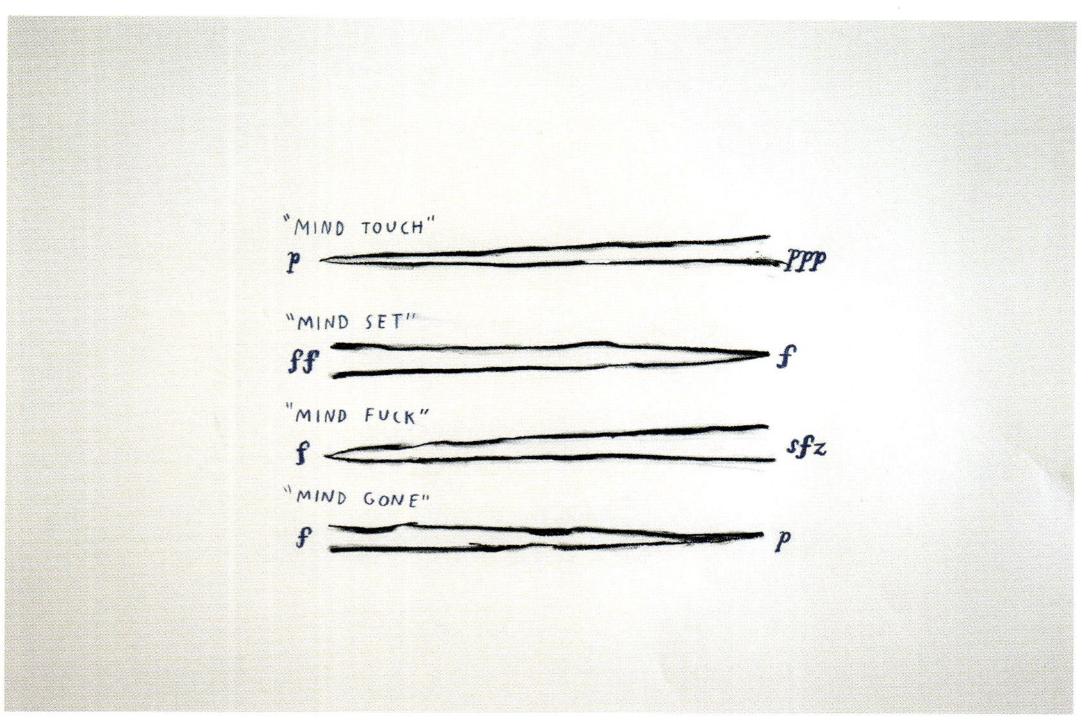

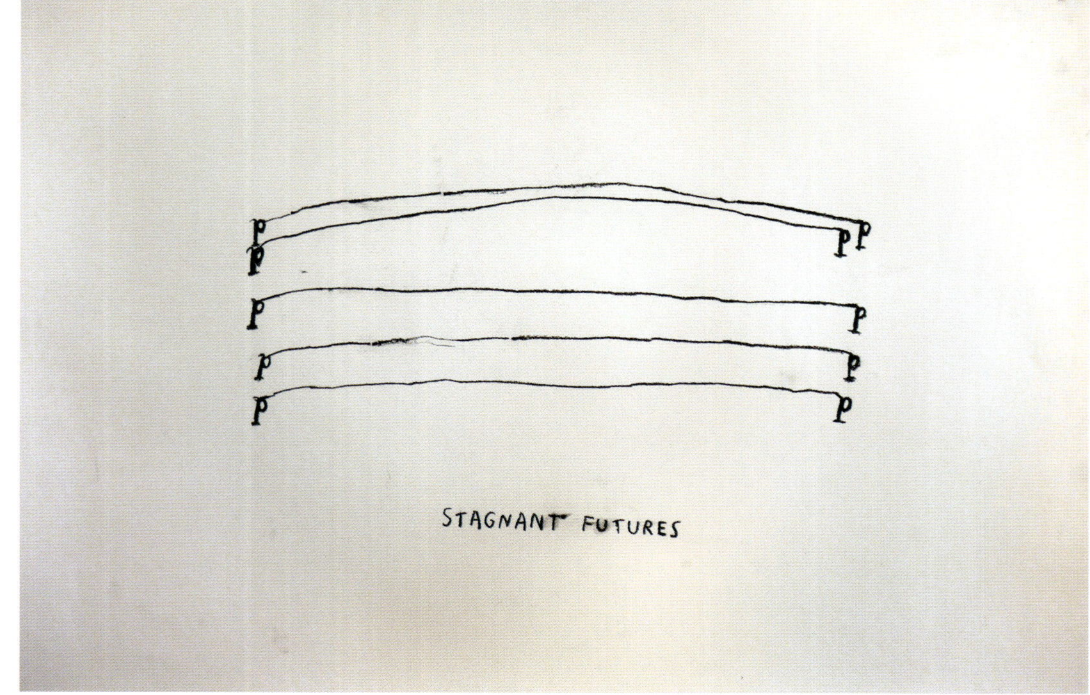

Four Stages, dry pastel and pencil on paper, 55 x 75cm, January 2016. Photograph Christine Sun Kim

Stagnant Futures, dry pastel and pencil on paper, 29.7 x 42cm, January 2016. Photograph Christine Sun Kim

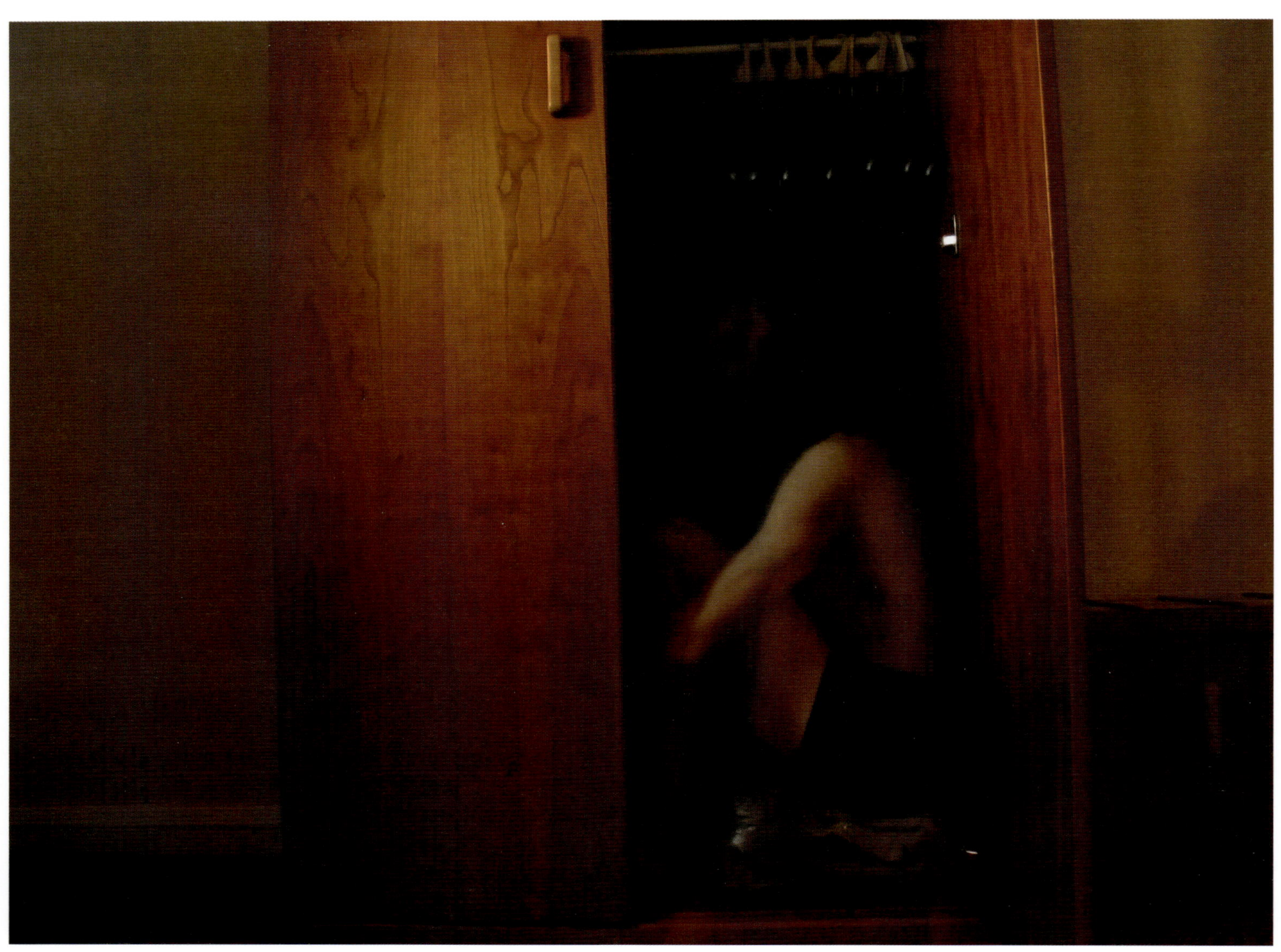

Çağlar Kimyoncu

A: I believe that you are born an artist, not inspired to become one. Whether or not you practice is another matter, but either way it's something that's within you already. I have always seen myself as an artist, it is the only way I can really *'communicate'*.

B: The biggest challenges I have encountered are hierarchies and power dynamics within the whole art scene, including the Disability Art movement itself. I am not sure if this is something I have overcome – those hierarchies still exist – but I think I've found ways to acknowledge these issues and continue working with them in mind. In general, I prefer to just keep creating rather than trying to fit in with a scene, and I have been fortunate enough to find like-minded creatives so far to work and collaborate with.

For me, the Disability Art scene is like a mirror: you don't always like what you see, but you learn to accept and work with it. A lot of work that I have done as part of collaborations has been recognised and supported through the Disability Art movement, while my own work has taken more time to be included and accepted. But that said, we do need the Disability Art scene, because we need safe and supported spaces in which to grow and support each other. That understanding and support system doesn't exist anywhere else.

C: I'm not sure whether to call myself a *'respected'* or *'established'* artist – these are quite subjective terms. I just keep creating and collaborating, being part of creative projects. We (myself and artists I collaborate with) do what we do, and trust our work will find its audience.

So I don't look to mainstream arts to measure my success, and I have no particular negative or positive feelings about the mainstream. *'Mainstream'* is a very fluid concept and changes based on different agendas. It's something I recognise but don't work with or

left: *Self Portrait Three,* digital photograph. Photograph Çağlar Kimyoncu

below: *Conscription,* HD Video, 2013. Stills diptych from *Conscription* (A Four Channel Installation – Funded by Arts Council England). Photograph Markus A. Ljungberg

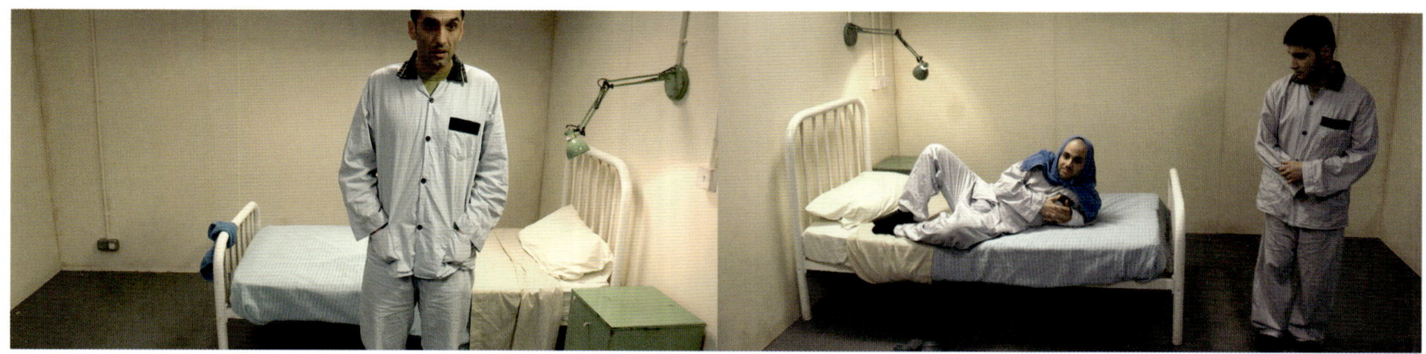

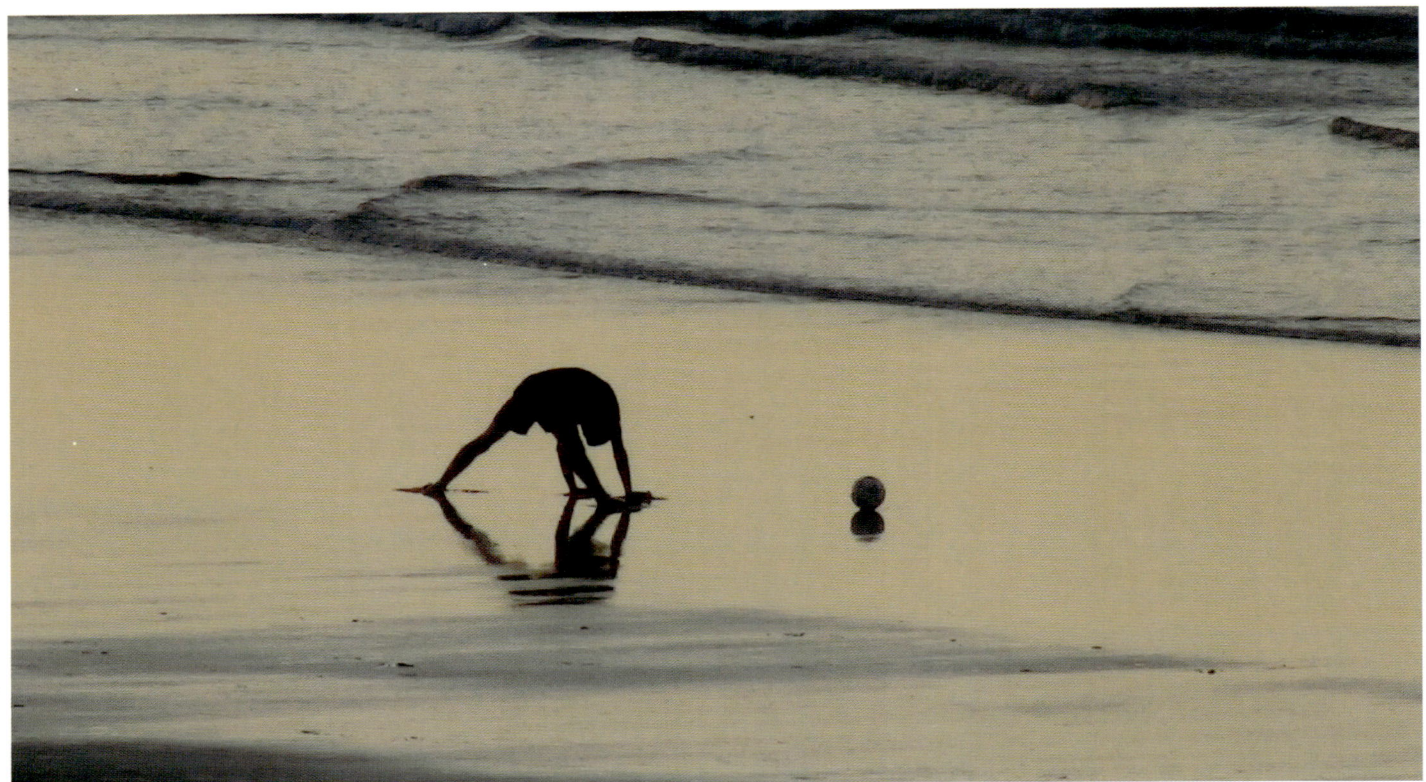

against. I feel more as though I co-exist with it, and occasionally might cross over into it.

D/E: I'm a creative person who enjoys being in creative environments – that's how I see and define myself. From the outside, it seems to help people to see me as a disabled, queer artist from a non-white, so-called 'ethnic minority' background. Coming from a straight, White European point of view, these labels define me as being *'different'* or *'other'*. But however they are described, I believe all these different aspects affect the way I see the world and approach my practice, and that being disabled, queer and Turkish are important components of my strength and political identity.

above: *At Kaza Beach,* digital photograph, 2011. Photograph Çağlar Kimyoncu

right: *Dance* (Giant Leap Festival), digital photograph, 2005. Photograph Çağlar Kimyoncu

F: My advice to emerging Disabled artists? Keep pushing the envelope. Use your courage to keep questioning. Seek out people you can communicate with, who will support you, and whom you can support as well. Embrace who you are, but don't let others define you – you are who you choose to be. Most importantly, keep creating!

caglark.com

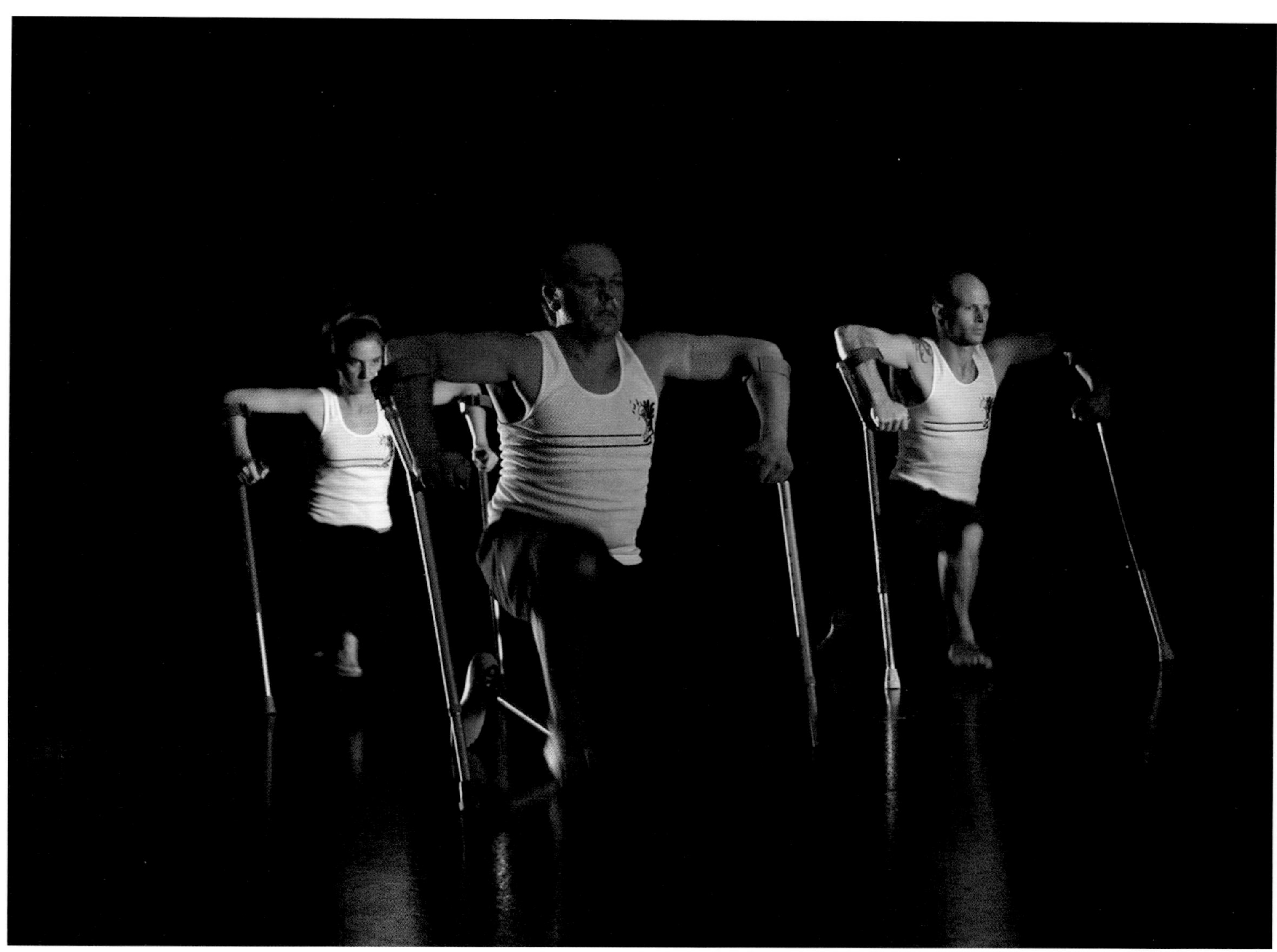

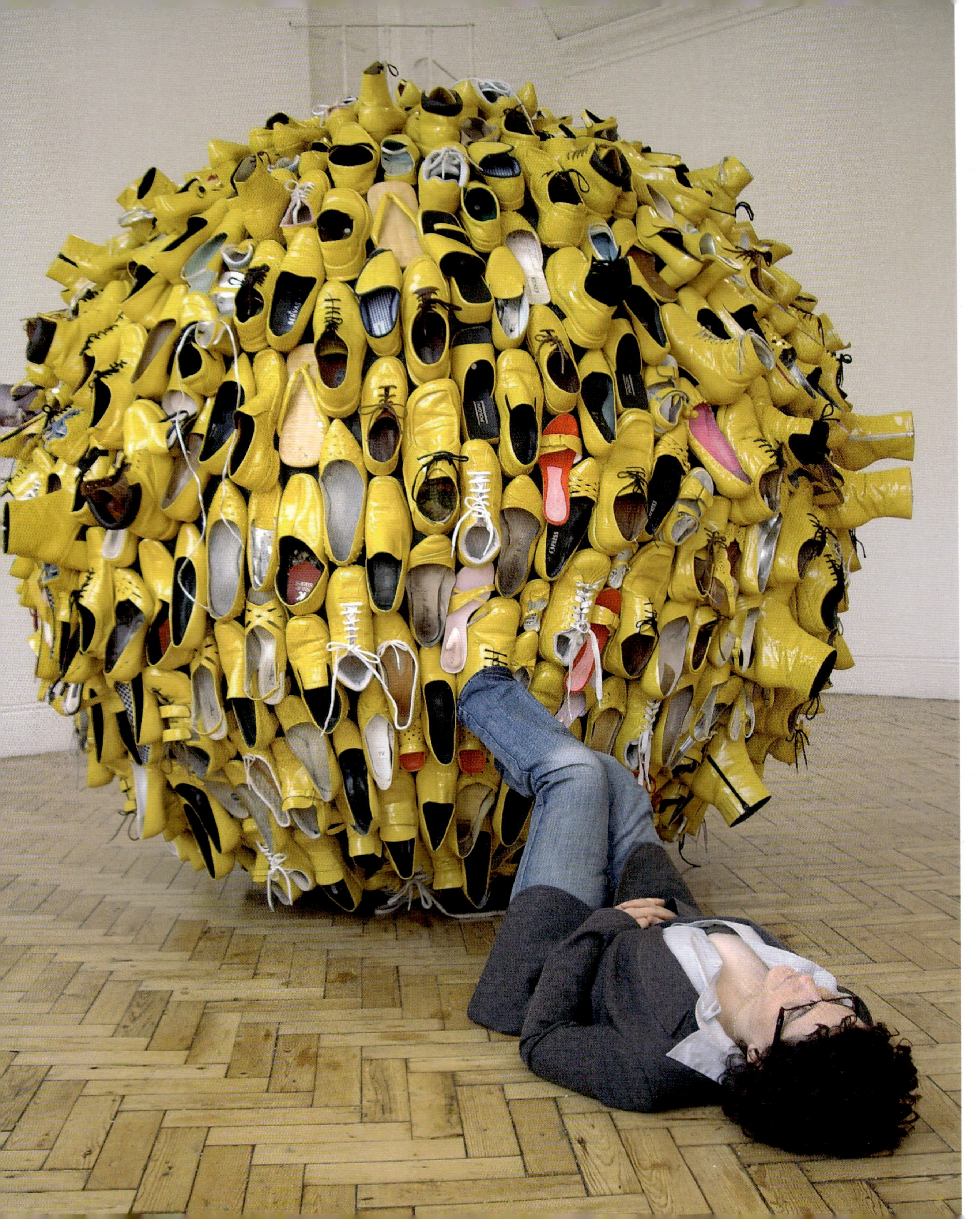

Noëmi Lakmaier

A: As I ponder over the question of what or who inspired me to become an artist, I find myself not knowing the answer; it feels like I have always known; always been. It has always felt like both a certainty and a need, a need for a language that has no words, to express that which cannot be said in any other way and that defies translation, because if it could be translated, it would not have needed an alternative language at all. I have always been fascinated by artists whose work I could innately understand but was unable to explain. I guess the possibility of being able to express myself like that inspired me to be an artist.

B: I think this is also the reason why I don't recall many obstacles and challenges, aside from occasional logistic and financial ones, in my early career. I had the certainty, of maybe youth or inexperience or whatever, that this is not just what I did, but who I was and that not doing this would in essence equate to not being, and was thus not an option. For me philosophical challenges, if I can call it that, came later, with reflection and with success. What does it mean to be an artist, and more frighteningly what would it mean not to be an artist?

C: What does it mean to be established/respected? Is it the euphoric highs that come with showing work in so-called mainstream venues in the establishment? Is it how many hits my name gets in a google search? Is it being invited to participate in shows and take up residencies? I love all this, and I feel I have been very fortunate to have had the opportunities and experiences I have had: A great art education at Winchester School of Art, that gave me the freedom, the space and the facilities to experiment with big installations; My brilliant residency at the Camden Arts Centre though the Adam Reynolds bursary; stints abroad in Ireland, the USA and Germany; and of course the wonderful support I have had and people I have met through organisations like LADA, ArtsAdmin, Shape, mac Birmingham and others.

The more 'established' I have become the less certain I have become. I increasingly feel a need to ground myself in the 'that-I-am' rather than the 'what-I-am' and what I have achieved, to then go back my profession as an artist with conviction and authenticity.

D: Disability Arts has played a major role in my journey to where I am now. I know for certain that I would not be where I am now without it. I was suspicious about it at first, scared that it would want to swallow me up and spit me out into a tightly sealed shoebox. In hindsight my early encounters with the 'Disability Arts movement' were disingenuous, I wanted the opportunities but I did not want to be identified with it. My stance has changed dramatically. I do not feel shoe-boxed, but rather taken out of

left: *Experiment in Happiness,* mixed media performance object, duration variable, 200 x 200 x 200cm + artist's body, 2008. Created during a Camden Arts Centre Residency as part of the Adam Reynolds Memorial Bursary. Photograph Hannah Facey

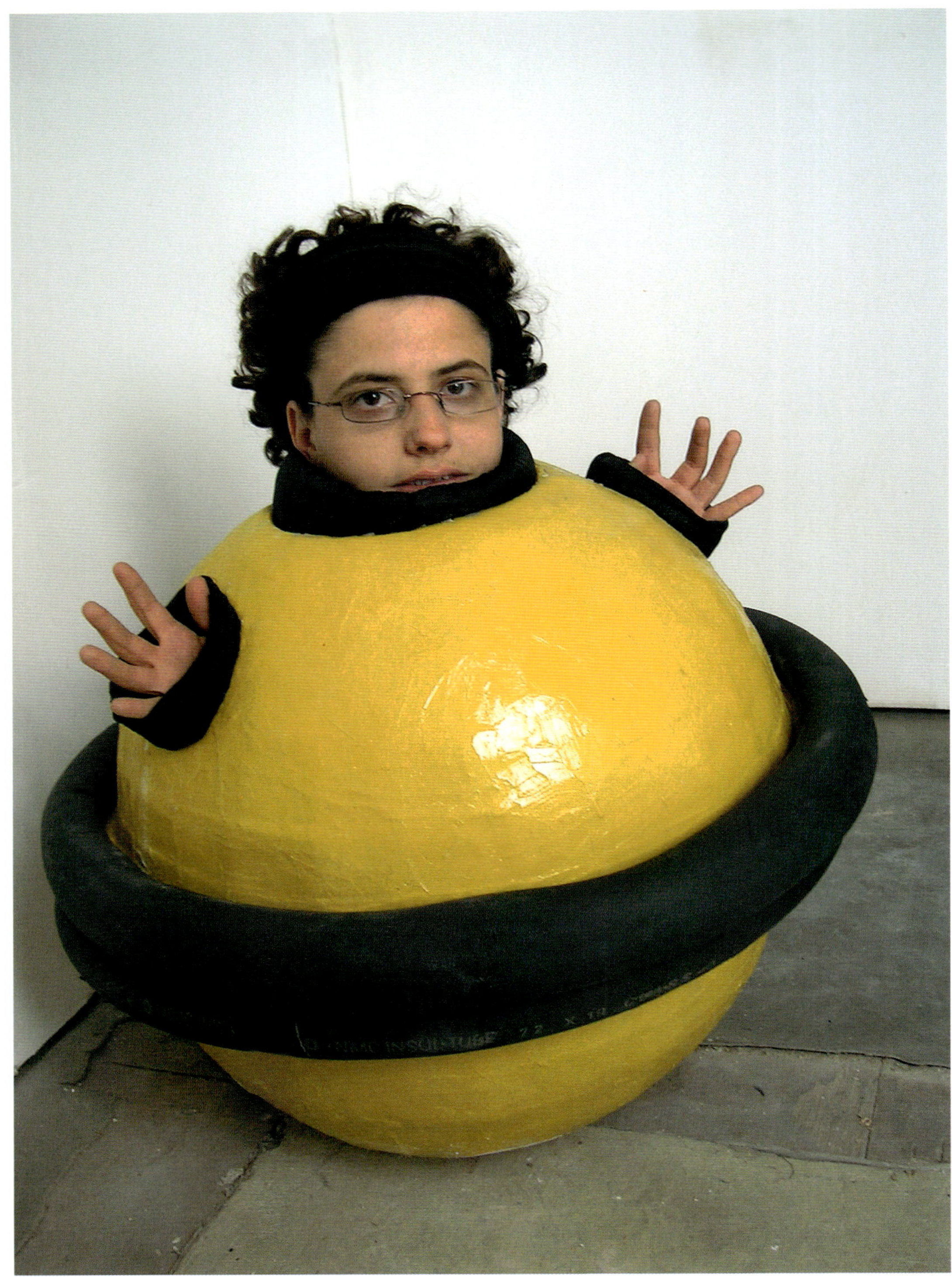

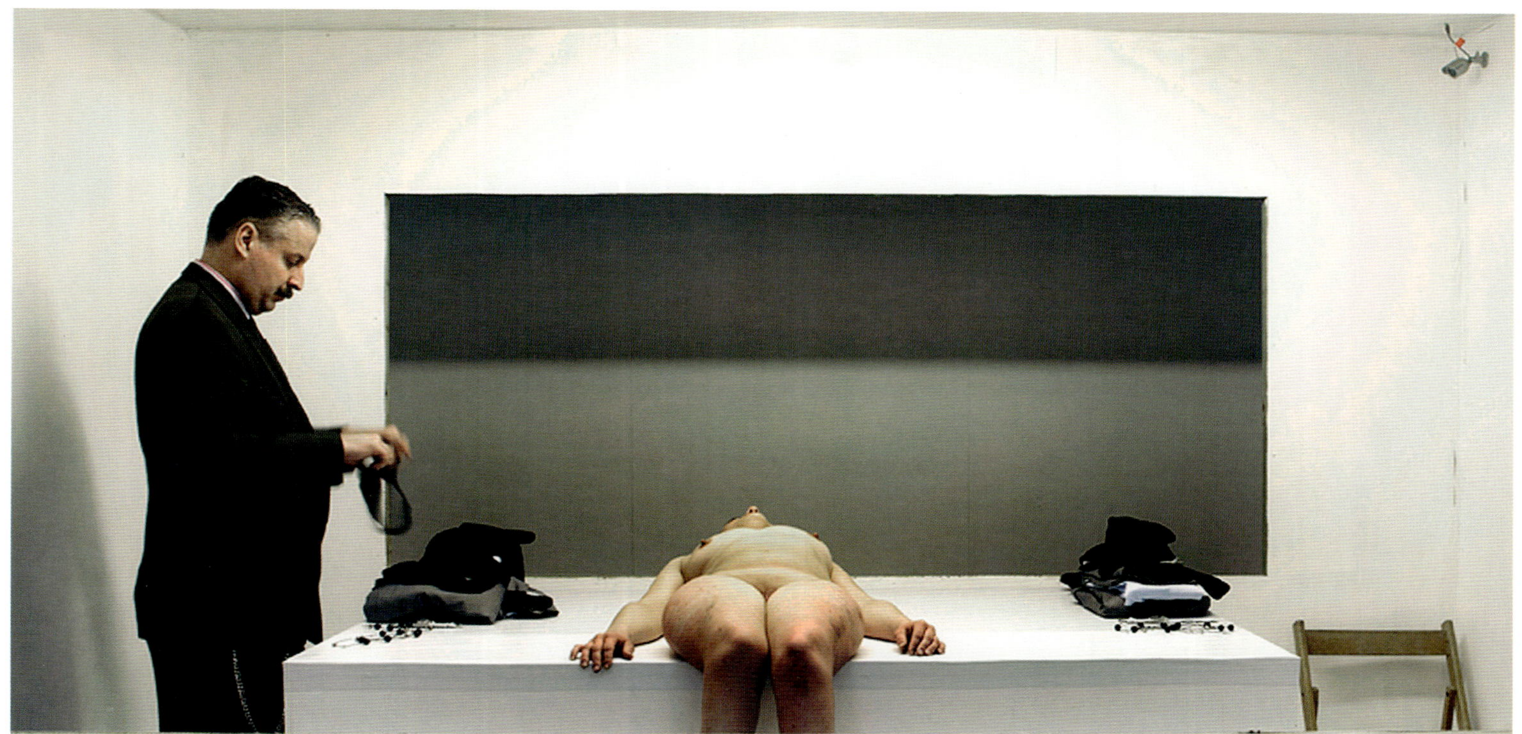

the box and liberated to be who or whatever I want and need to be, to define myself rather than be defined as 'other' by the 'other'.

E: I tend to avoid binary identification. I am first and foremost human and everything else is flexible and subject to change. I sometimes identify as a Disabled artist and sometimes as simply an artist, sometimes I identify in other ways, a woman, a student, a psychotherapist,

left: *Exercise in Loosing Control,* mixed media performance object, duration 4 hours, 55 x 55 x 55cm + artist's body, 2007. Photograph Joy Stanley

above: *Undress Re-dress,* performance installation, duration variable, 2011. Commissioned by the Live Arts Development Agency for Access All Areas – Live Art and Disability. Photograph Manuel Vason

a friend. I cannot stand labels and yet I am labeled and label myself all the time. I just don't like any of these labels to be too sticky, so that I can swap them and change them, take them all off or wear them all at the same time.

F: I find it hard to give advice to younger Disabled (or non-disabled) artists, as there is a risk that they might follow it. I cannot enter their world, which inherently means my advice might be wrong for them. I think the best thing I can say is: Try to be as best as you can, to be who you are, and accept that this will change over time. Talk to people, find what feels right for you. Have a laugh and a pint every now and again.

www.noemilakmaier.co.uk

Simon Mckeown

A: The artistic process was innate. From a young age I was drawn into making things, which I felt was the correct thing to do. I was also helped along the way by other factors. My senior school wasn't the most pleasant place to be with a disability. I was subject to a lot of bullying, which was endemic and included violence. My art classes, as a result, stood out: the teachers engaged the students successfully. Pivotally, my art teachers at Sixth Form College and on my Foundation Course were dedicated and inspiring. They helped make sense of my artistic aspirations, assessing and supporting me very well, whilst steering my direction and skills development in the way that memorable teachers can do.

B: I have had to look after myself and to consider from an early age how to create work that engaged me and, I hoped, would engage others. Months of broken bones led to isolation, movement limitation, experiential reduction, and motor loss. This simply focused me. I was quite clear that I would work in the creative industries and achieving that goal, becoming a fine artist, really did become paramount. My imagination ruled my world because, to a large extent, it was the main thing I relied on as my own personal support network! I was also encouraged by my family, who supported my artistic endeavours.

C: I have a very good relationship with all of the galleries and producers I have worked with. The creative industries are a difficult professional area to access. Funding and opportunities are always an issue and it's still immensely challenging. I work with both a short-term and a very long-term view and really enjoy the projects that I work to create.

D: The Disability Art movement has provided inspiration in the form of artworks, artists, and as a support network to me for the last 15 years. I no longer exist solely; rather, my work and its context can be considered by my constituents,

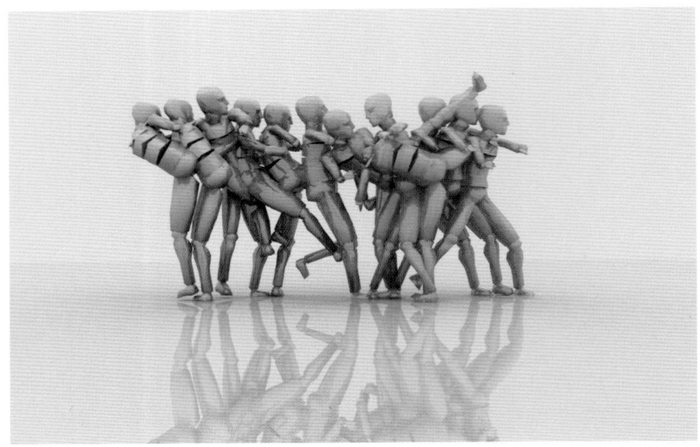

Motion Disabled, 2009 exhibition relating to disabled motion capture, digital images and animation, 15 minutes of motion capture looped across multiple TV screens. Supported by Wellcome Trust and Teesside University. Image: Digital render by Simon Mckeown. www.motiondisabled.com

right: *Cork Ignite,* large-scale outdoor projection based public performance, duration 30 minutes, Sept 18 2015. Cork City Centre, Ireland, as part of Culture Night Ireland, with support from Teesside University and XL Video. Cork Ignite was led by the National Sculpture Factory and Create Ireland in association with SoundOUT and Suisha Inclusive Arts at COPE Foundation. Cork Ignite was commissioned by Cork City Council as part of Ignite. Ignite is managed by a unique partnership involving the Arts Council, Arts & Disability Ireland (AD), Cork City Council, Galway City and County Councils and Mayo County Council. Photograph Clare Keogh

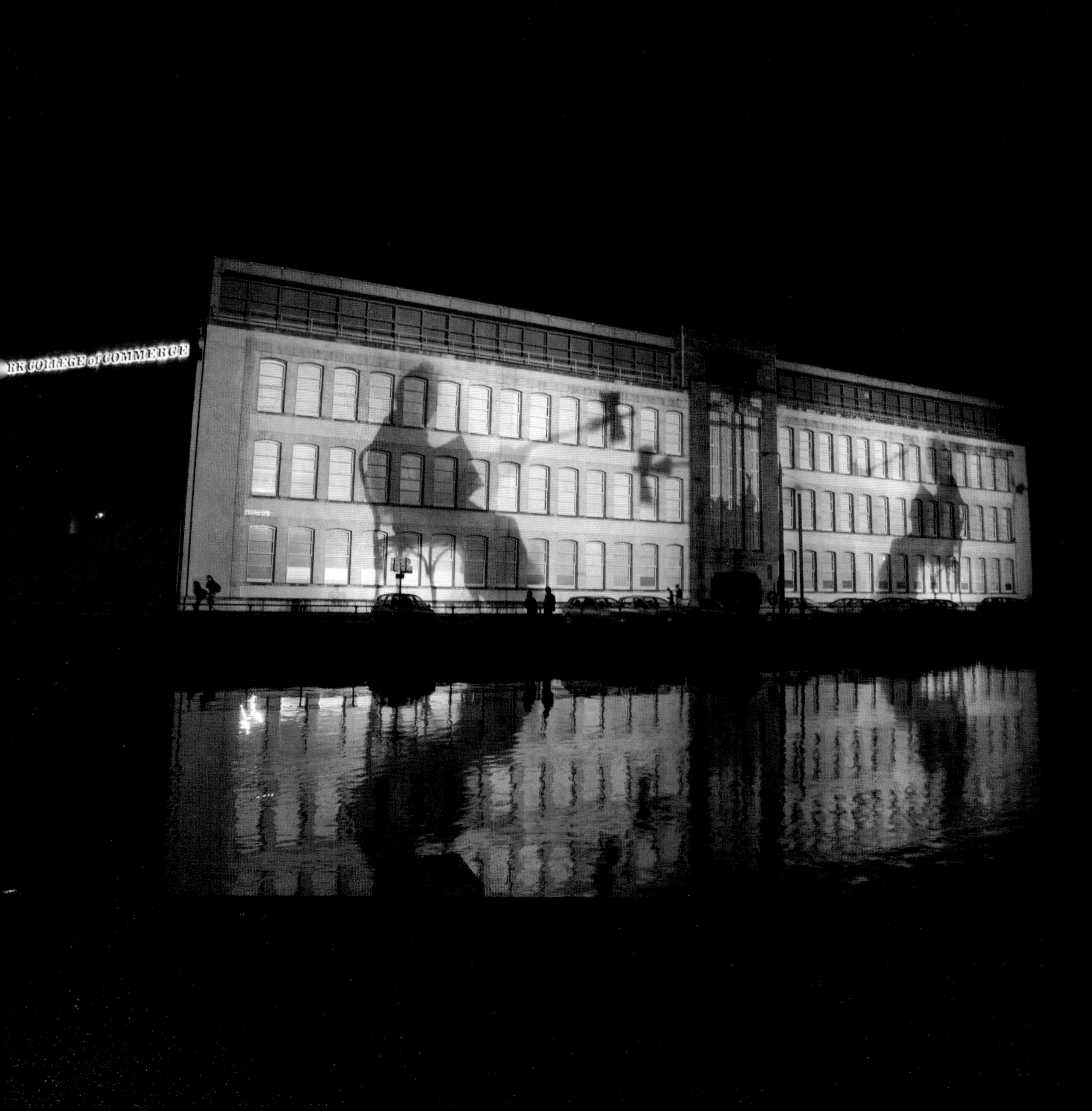

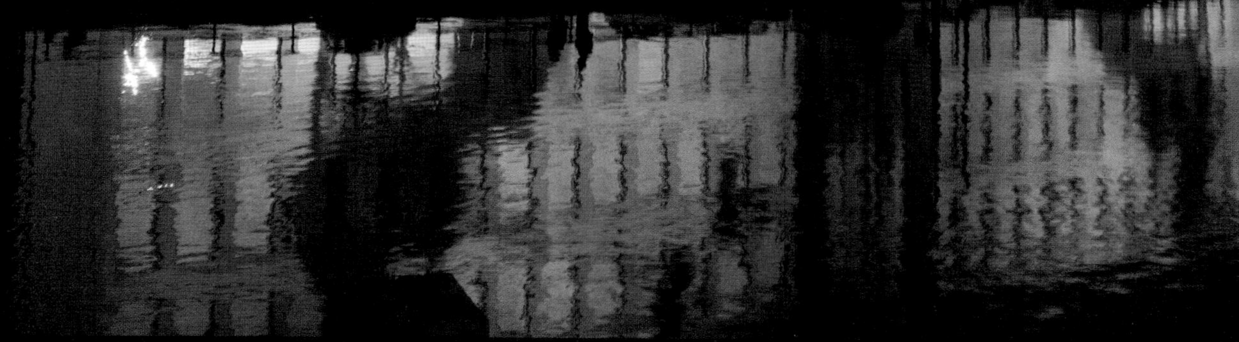
RK COLLEGE of COMMERCE

i.e., by other people who have lived disability, as well as by the population as a whole. My work has been supported and adopted by the Disability Arts movement, too. For instance, I was awarded DaDaFest Artist of the Year in 2010 in Liverpool, for my work *Motion Disabled.*

E: The Disability Art movement is simply part of my life. Art and disability are part of who I am. The movement provides a cognitive, academic, and professional explanation for my work, both to me and, I hope, to the 20% of the population who have or will acquire a disability in their lifetime. I am a Disabled artist and am confident enough in my work to be identified, where appropriate, in this way.

F: Many things affect the success of an artist. Effort, patience, intelligent work, marketing approaches, and a method of developing your own contacts and support network are critical. It's a hugely challenging area for all artists. Class, location, and disability can have a positive or negative effect; however, there are almost no rules, which also is immensely positive – and Disabled artists have some of the best stories to tell. Go for it!

www.simon-mckeown.com

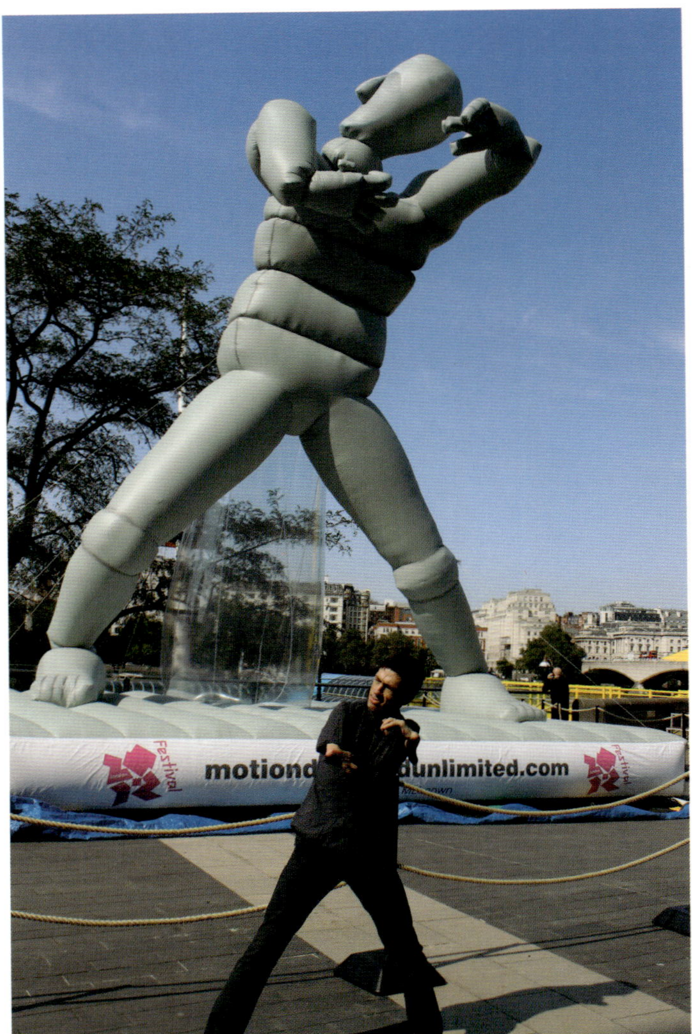

top: *Motion Disabled Unlimited* – Mat Fraser with inflatable sculpture. Large-scale outdoor inflatable sculpture, 10 x 4 x 3m, Summer 2012. London 2012 Festival commission supported by Arts Council England and Teesside University. Photograph Iain Jacques. www.motiondisabledunlimited.com

right: *Prometheus Awakes,* large-scale outdoor digital projection and public performance, 45 Minutes, 2nd August 2012. Video design and projection by Simon Mckeown. Stockton International Riverside Festival – Prometheus Awakes was co-commissioned by GDIF and SIRF. Photograph Spencer Hudson. www.simon-mckeown.com/out-door-projection

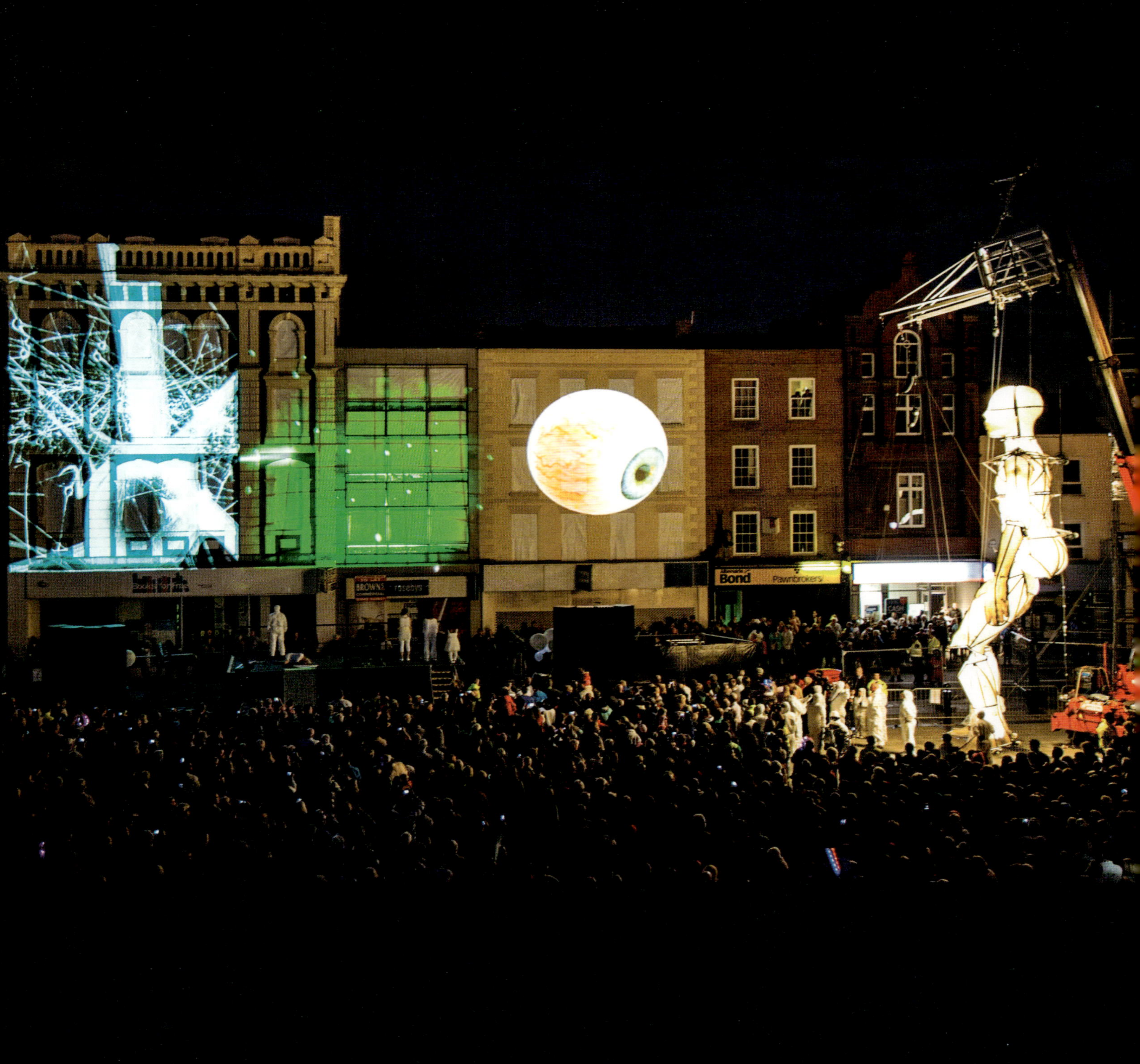
BROWNS
rosebys
Bond
Pawnbrokers

Cameron Morgan

A: I've always done art of some sort, I started doing it in the hospital school when I was just a laddie. One of the art teachers used to bring stuffed animals to draw with charcoal and pencils. I like Mackintosh, Van Gogh and Gaudi, and Salvador Dali and his sculptures. I like nature. I like art that you can see the person has put a lot of work into it.

B: I just used to do art in house, but nobody really looks at it and you are limited in the scale and size of work you can do. I attended a day centre and there wasn't much to do, and there was always noise. They did cooking and gardening and sports, which is fine if you are into that. In the early nineties I started at Project Ability, over the years I started to come in most days. I started doing ceramics and a big mosaic thing 'Let Peace Flourish'. I've been to Ireland twice, Denmark, the low countries, and Germany with Steven Reilly. If it wasn't for Project Ability I wouldn't have had so many opportunities. People get to see my work and buy it. I've learned new skills and I like the people here, they are good fun.

C: I like going to see different things that catch your eye. I like looking at sculpture. I don't like abstract, I'm not a big fan. If people put a lot of effort making something, then I like it. It's how it's done. I like Angel of the North. I like detail, not blandness. The golden rule is I like seeing something how it's meant to be.

D: One thing I have noticed is that you don't see a lot of Disabled artists on TV or in movies.

below: *Having Supper,* oil pastel on paper, 100 x 240cm, 2016. Photograph Berengere Chabonois

right: *Zorro,* acrylic on canvas, 120 x 160cm, 2016. Commissioned by Unlimited. Photograph Berengere Chabonois

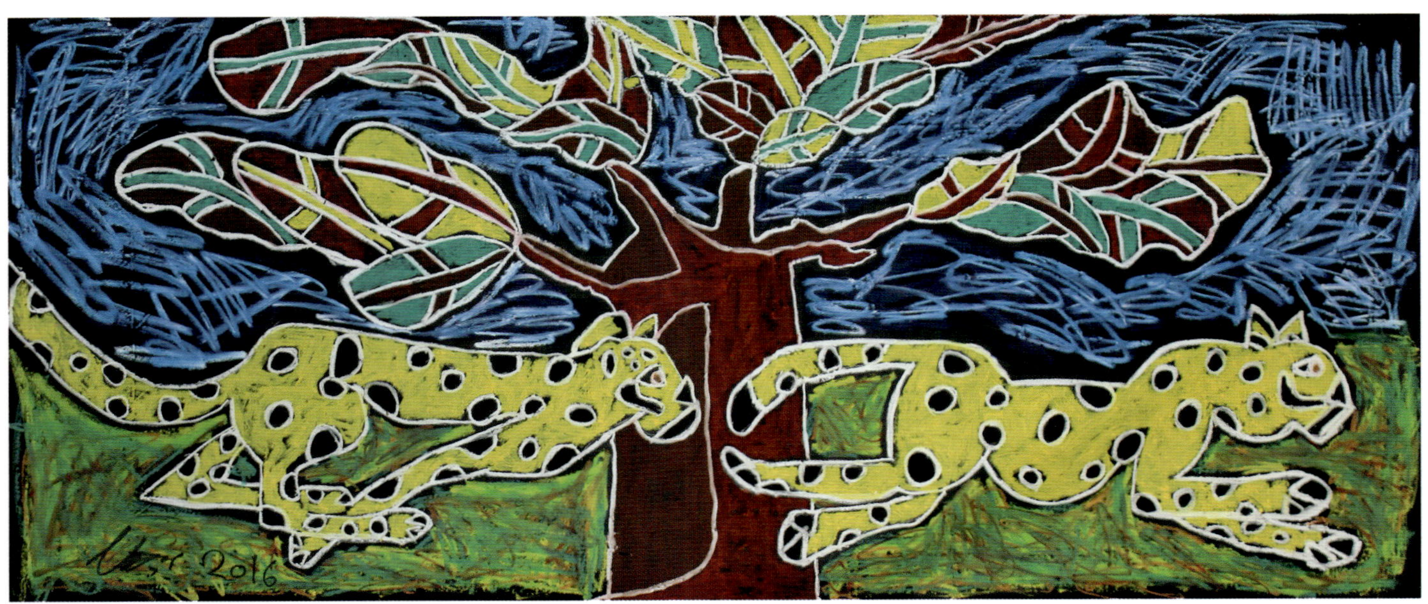

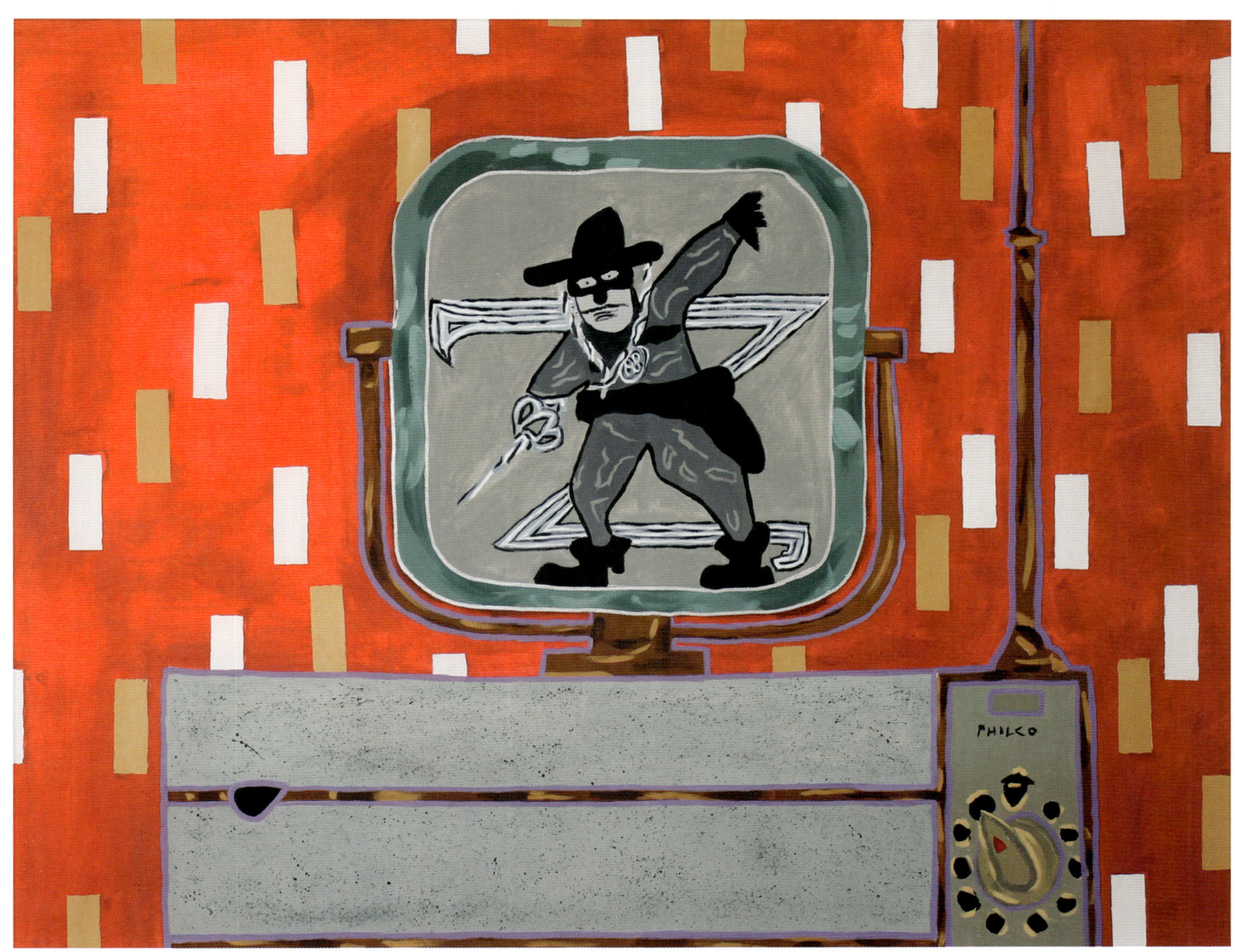
PHILCO

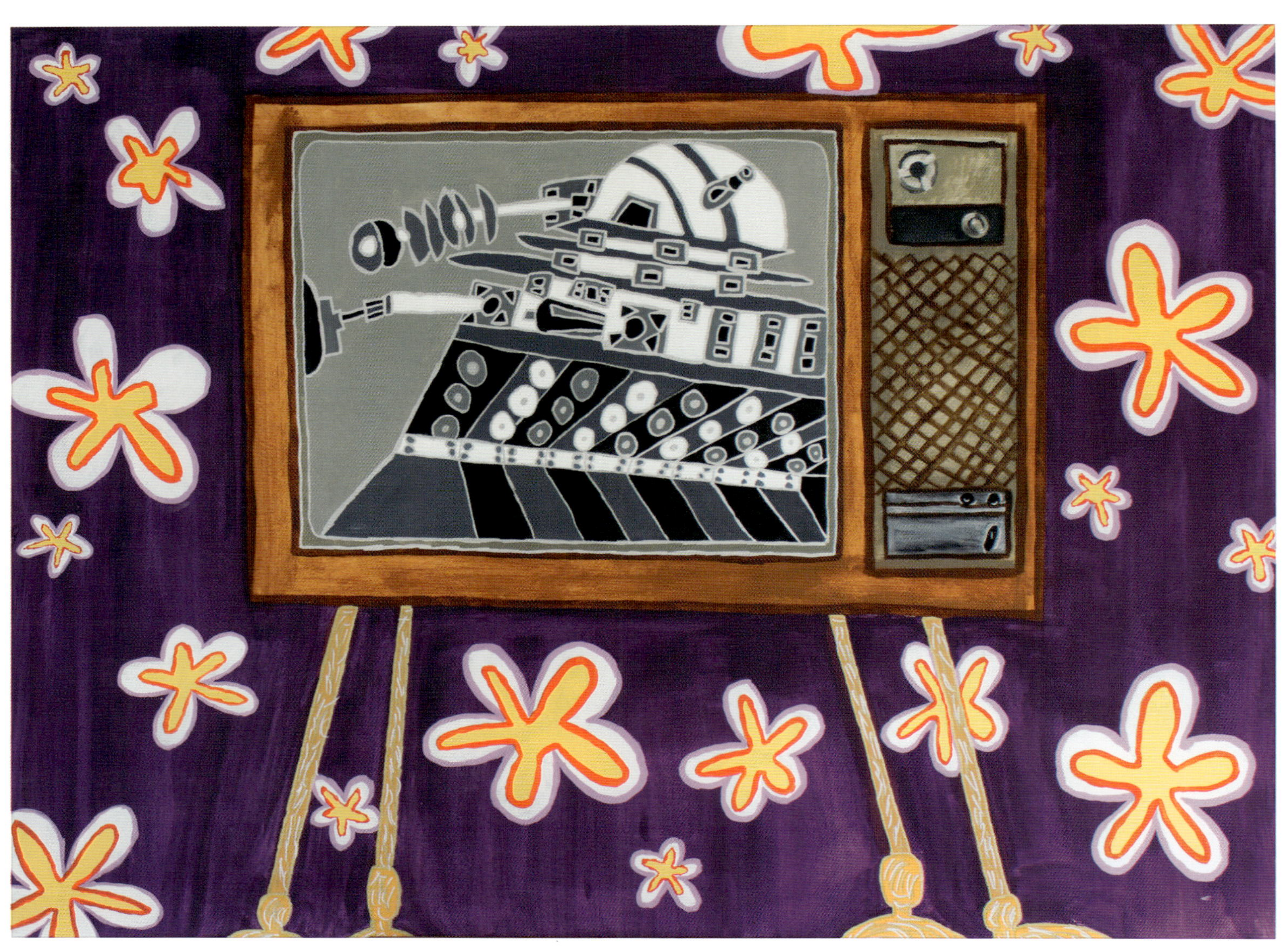

above: *Dr Who,* acrylic on canvas, 120 x 160cm, 2016.
Commissioned by Unlimited. Photograph Berengere Chabonois

right: *Breakfast,* ceramic, 30 x 50 x 5cm, 2015.
Photograph Berengere Chabonois

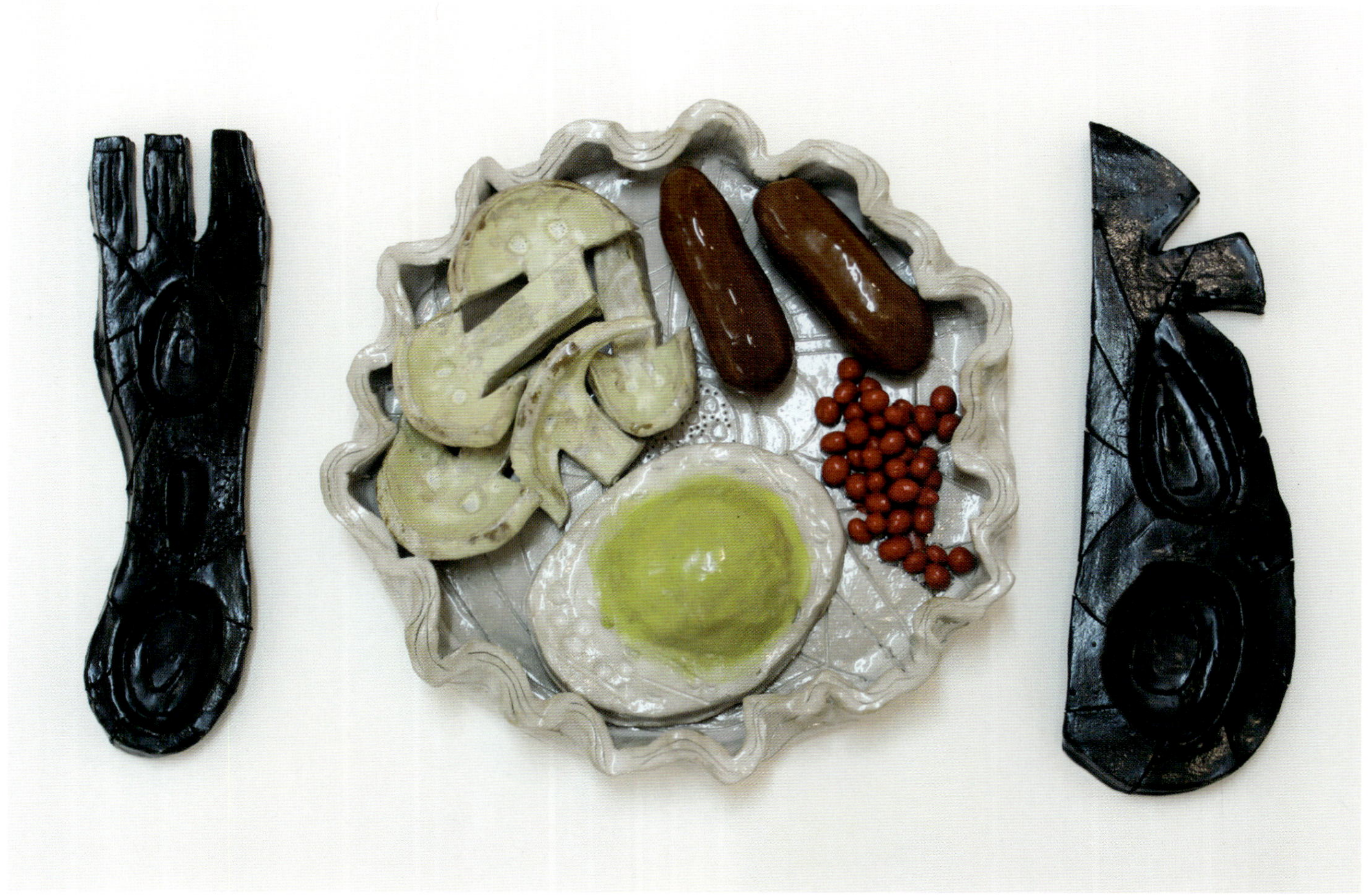

A lot of Disabled people are not good readers or writers, it's a struggle to find somewhere to go to make art. It's hard for a Disabled artist to make a living out of art and to make art. A lot of Disabled artists are on benefits, transport costs money, getting around can be hard work. A lot of work by Disabled artists doesn't get seen. Without Project Ability I would struggle. You need organisations like Project Ability for opportunities to exhibit. When it comes to funding it's not my strong point, I need people to know how to go about it. I'm just as good as any artist out there, I give it everything I have, I give it one hundred percent.

E: I'm passionate, I like what I do. I'm not bad at what I do, I'm quite good. When it comes to disability I don't give it a good deal of thought.

F: I would say stick with what you are good at and give it 100 percent. Always learn new things. If anything comes your way always take the opportunity.

www.project-ability.co.uk
www.tvclassicspart1.co.uk

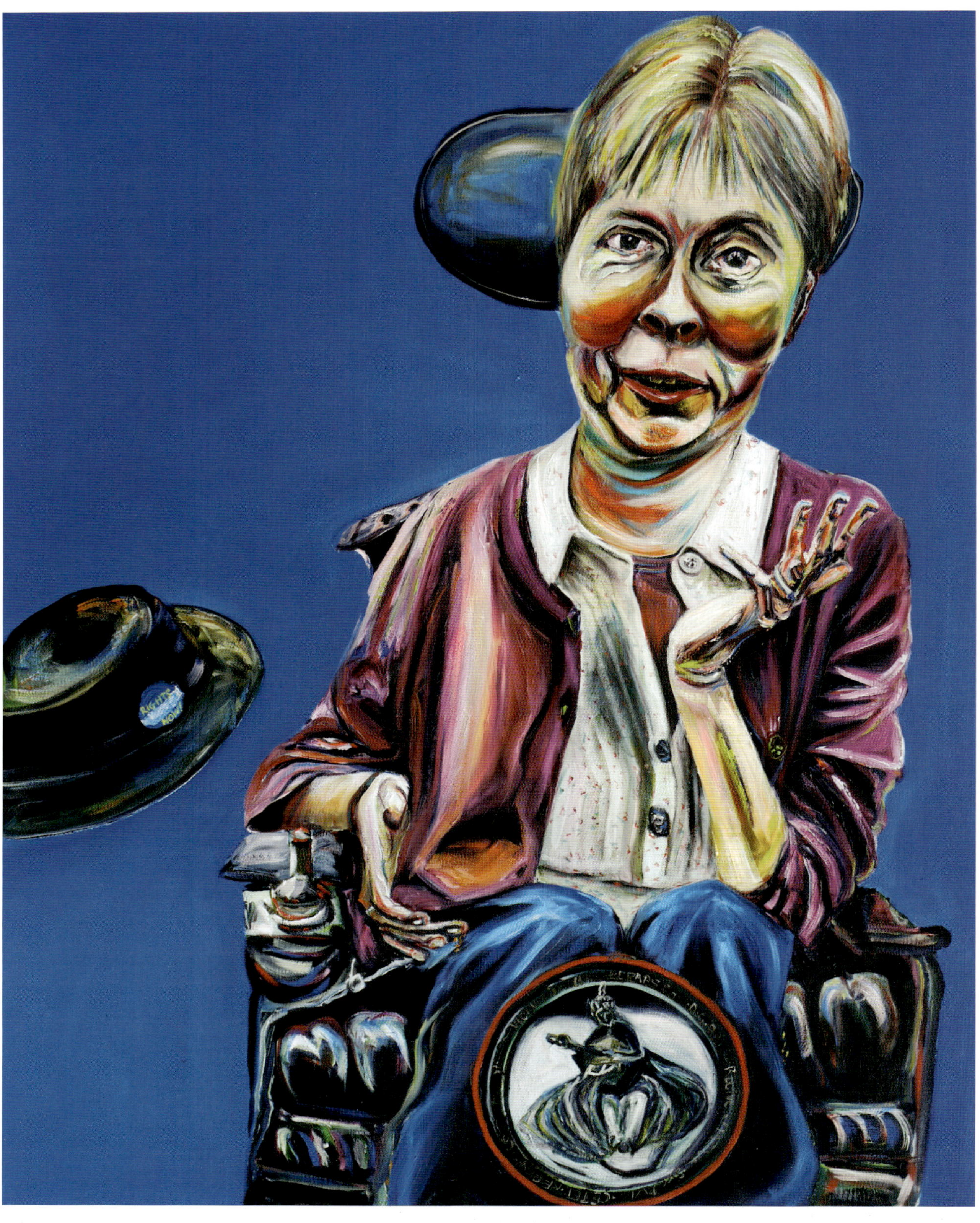
RIGHTS
NOW!

Tanya Raabe-Webber

A: I had an ambition to become an artist from a very early age. I went to a boarding school for Disabled children with an incredible range of impairments and the education was centred around being cared for and not at all academically inclined. Drawing was something I was good at and I was encouraged by the teachers and care staff. I won my first art competition at a school garden fete – a pencil drawing of the school house. And I've never looked back!

B: My main personal challenges were around fitting in. What art form and cultural perspective did my art work come from? I couldn't see any other art or artists who were making work from a disability cultural body politic. So I began a research project of my own. I wanted to find out where my work would be accepted and who would support it so I could make an informed choice as to which camp to follow. Disability Arts or mainstream?

I sent out a letter including images of my work that said I was a Disabled artist looking for exhibitions and another letter where I just said I was an artist looking for exhibitions, to both Disability Arts organisations and mainstream arts organisations.

The results were both fascinating and surprising. Disability Arts embraced me as a 'Disabled Artist' and dissed me as *'just an artist'*. The mainstream arts organisations just never replied! This was in the late 80s just as the revolution of Disability Arts movement was at its most politically active. So I guess you can see where I found myself fitting in and here began my career as a professional Disabled artist.

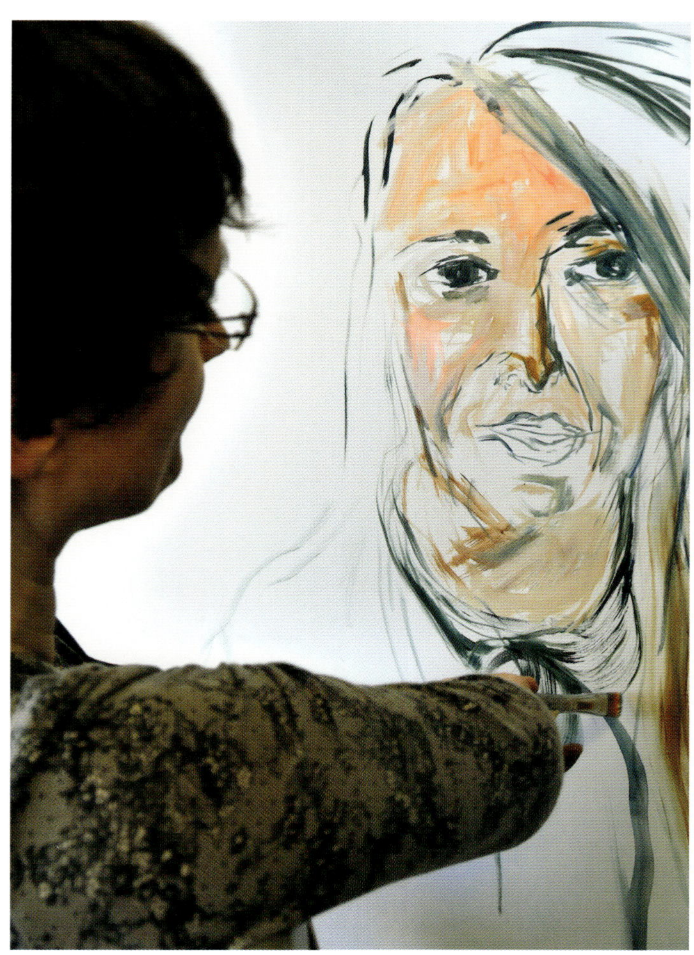

left: *Baroness Jane Campbell of Surbiton, D.B.E, Active Crossbench Peer in the House of Lords,* oil on canvas, 91.5 x 76cm, 2011. Baroness Jane Campell private collection. Photograph Tanya Raabe-Webber

right: *PortraitsUntold: Tanya Raabe-Webber portrays Dame Evelyn Glennie,* 2016. Photograph Tanya Raabe-Webber

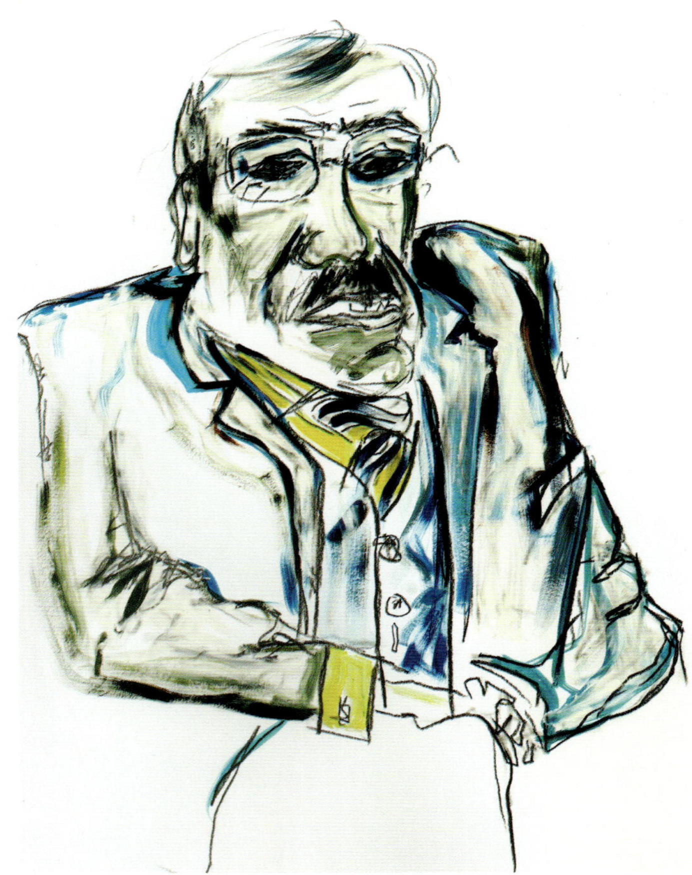

left: *Preliminary Sketch: Sir Bert Massie,* acrylic and ink on Fabriano, 59.5 x 84, 2010. Photograph Tanya Raabe-Webber

right: *Tony Heaton, sculptor/pioneer of NDACA,* oil on canvas, 91.5 x 76cm, 2007. National Disability Arts Collection and Archive at Holton Lee. Photograph Tanya Raabe-Webber

C: I find the so called mainstream art world to be a strange and wondrous beast. Sometimes it can be open, reflective and responsive to Disability Arts and cultural perspectives. When this happens it's like a breath of fresh air and the battles are no more. I love going into some of our world renowned art galleries and art institutions around the country, introducing them to the delights of a vibrant and diverse Disability Arts movement and seeing their eureka moment! Then figuring out with the organisations how to embed our art into their histories.

D: The Disability Arts movement has been fundamental in the making of my art and my career as a pioneering award winning Disabled artist. It has given me the structure and political constructs by which I make my work. I continue to this day to record and create portraits of high profile Disabled people and disability culture. May I never run out of subjects to paint!

E: I am borne out of the Disability Arts movement and self-identify as such, because my work predominantly comes from, and is informed by, my experiences as a Disabled woman, friend, artist, wife, sister, and daughter.

F: The best piece of advice I can offer you as an emerging artist is to be true to yourself and your art. Follow your dream, don't give up. Drive and ambition can be achieved if you stick at it. Surround yourself with positive people.

Ask for help when you need it, especially in the areas of your professional practice that you find difficult. Research is the key to discovering who you are as an artist, where your work should be exhibited and who you want to work with on what projects.

http://www.tanyaraabe.co.uk/
http://portraitsuntold.co.uk/

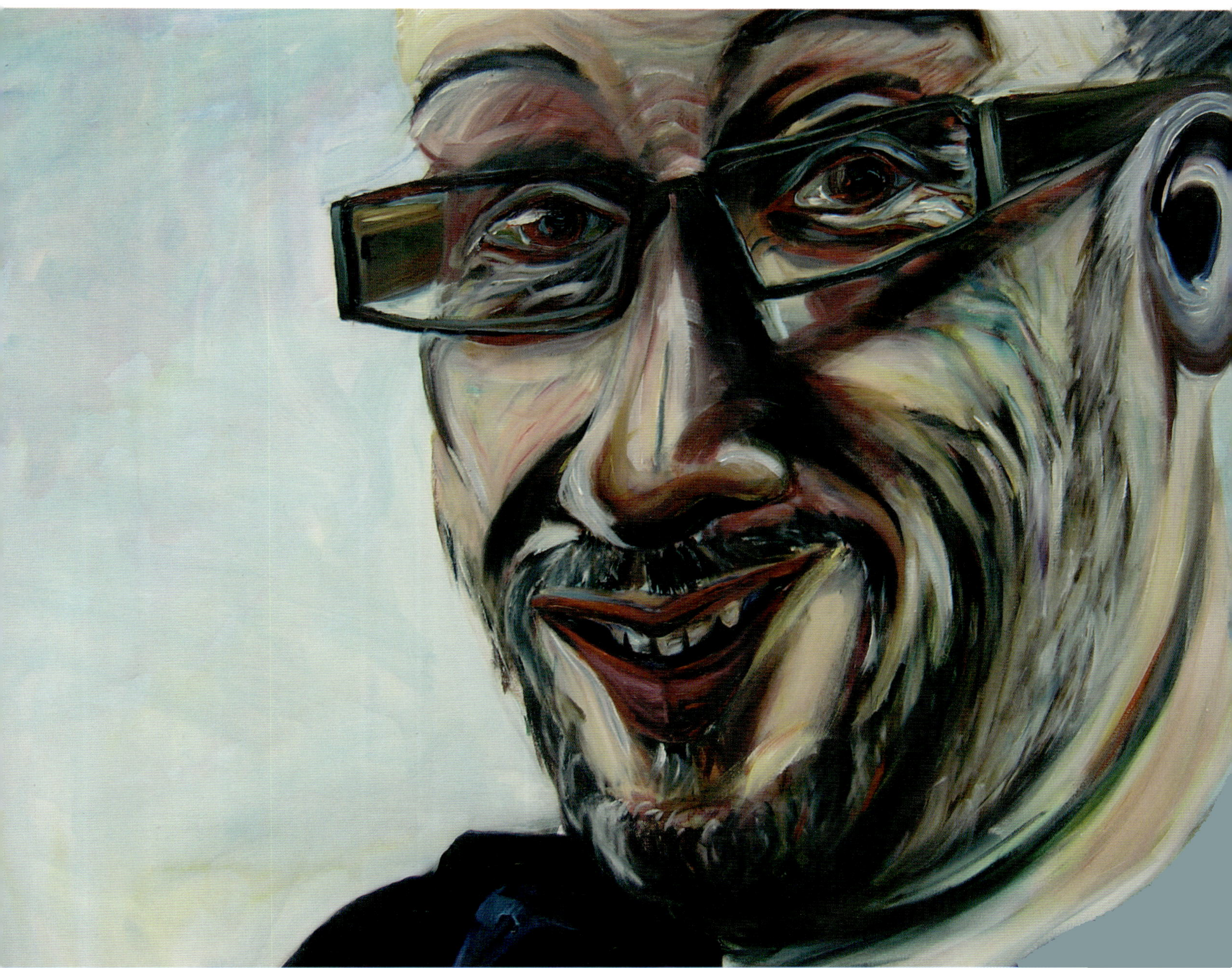

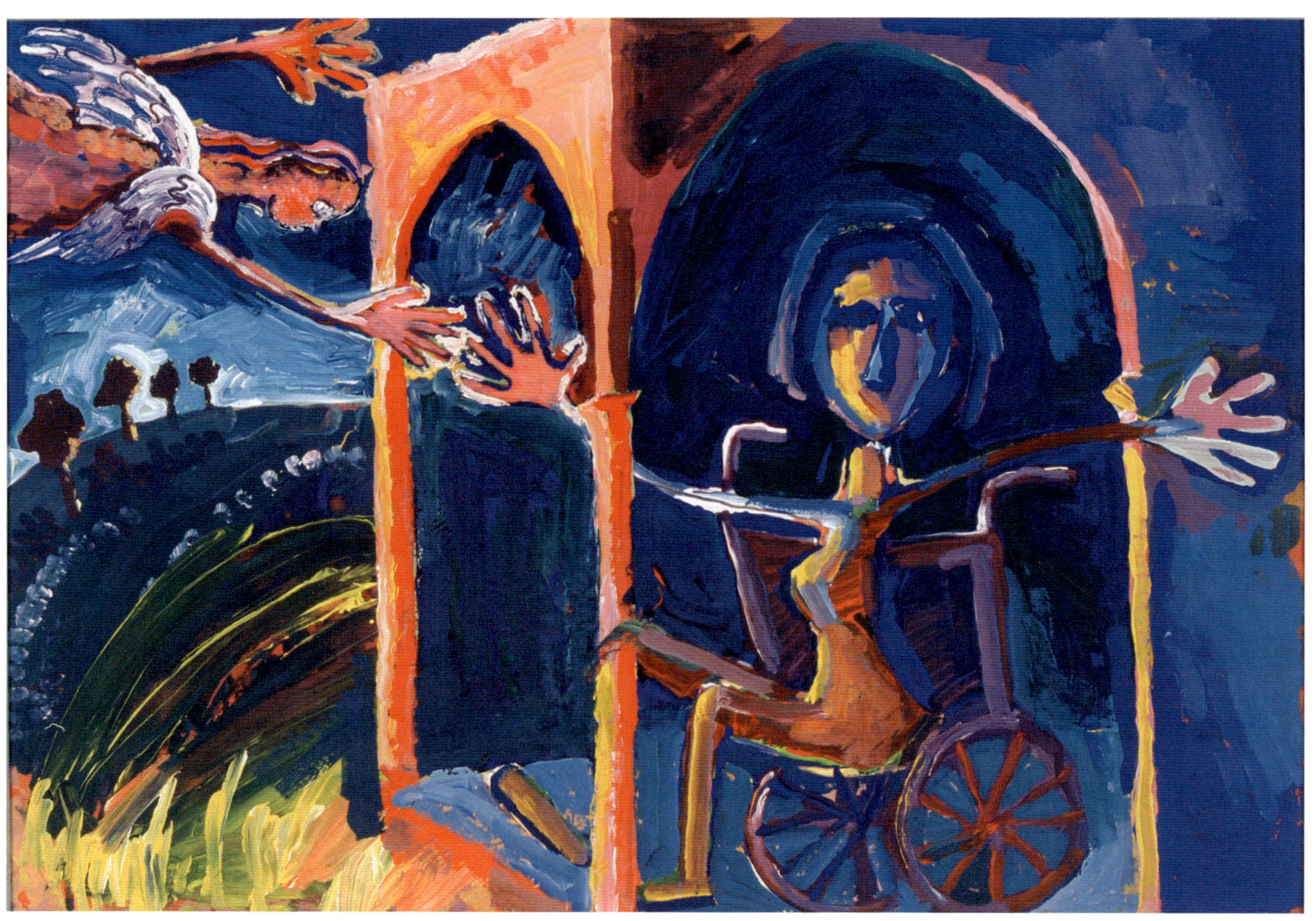

Nancy Willis

As a child I was adventurous: I ran about and played with my four brothers, dreaming of becoming an explorer, or joining the circus as a trapeze artist.

But as I grew up, I became gradually disabled by muscular dystrophy. I finished my education at a residential, 'special' school. By the time I left, I had had enough of rules and I was longing for freedom and adventure. One day, pondering on my unpromising future, somebody suggested art college, and I thought, yes, that will do for me. Yet it was not until some years after leaving college that I began to recognise that my art need not be about the kinds of things I saw in galleries, or what was current in the contemporary art world.

In the fairy stories of our childhood, physical perfection and beauty represented goodness, while imperfections and deformity were reserved for the wicked and cruel. In art history, Disabled people appeared as beggars, victims of war, or pitiful candidates for miraculous intervention.

Embarking on a series of self-portraits, I wanted to create new images of disability as a

left: *Annunciation,* gouache on paper, 60 x 80cm, 1994. Collection of Martha Prevezer and David Alberman

below: *Childhood,* digital photo montage, 14 x 26cm, 2016. Images from the Willis family album

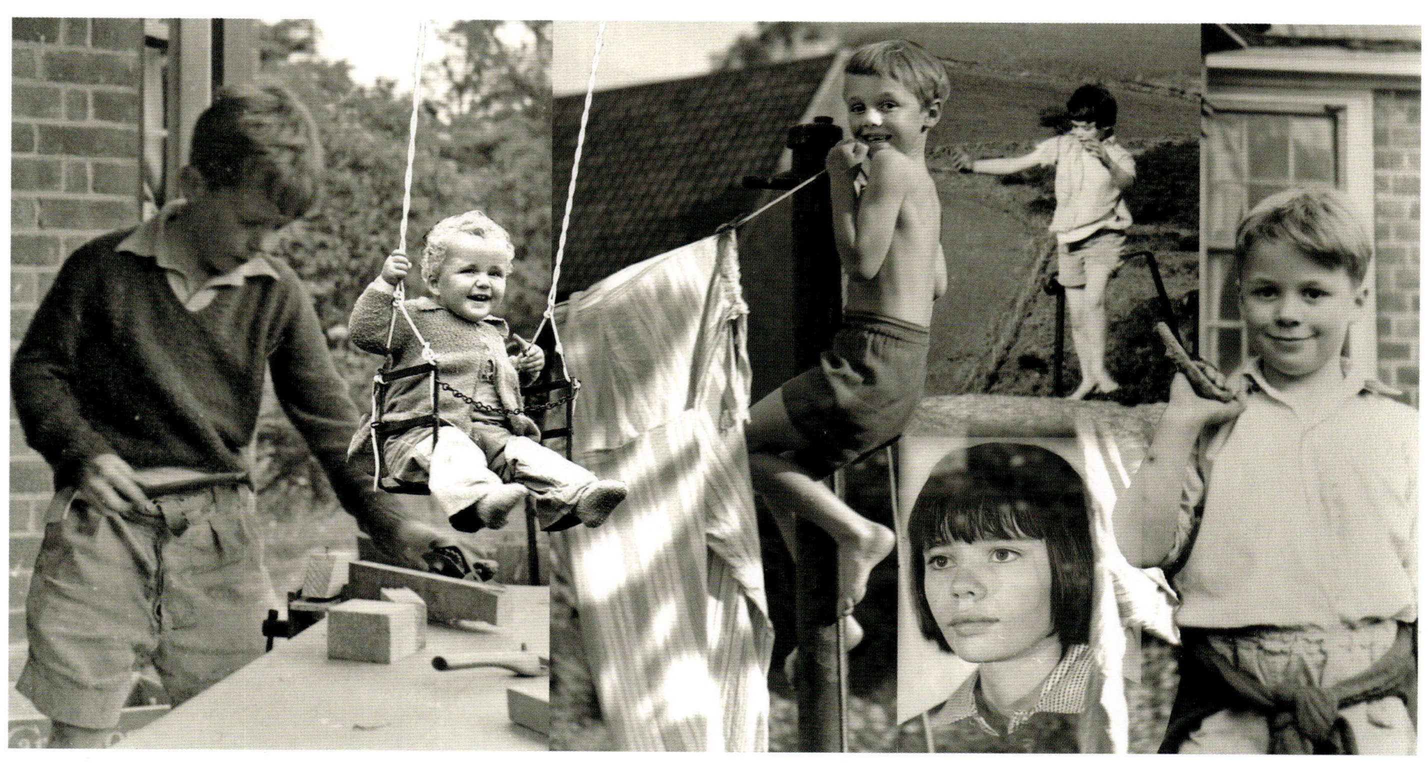

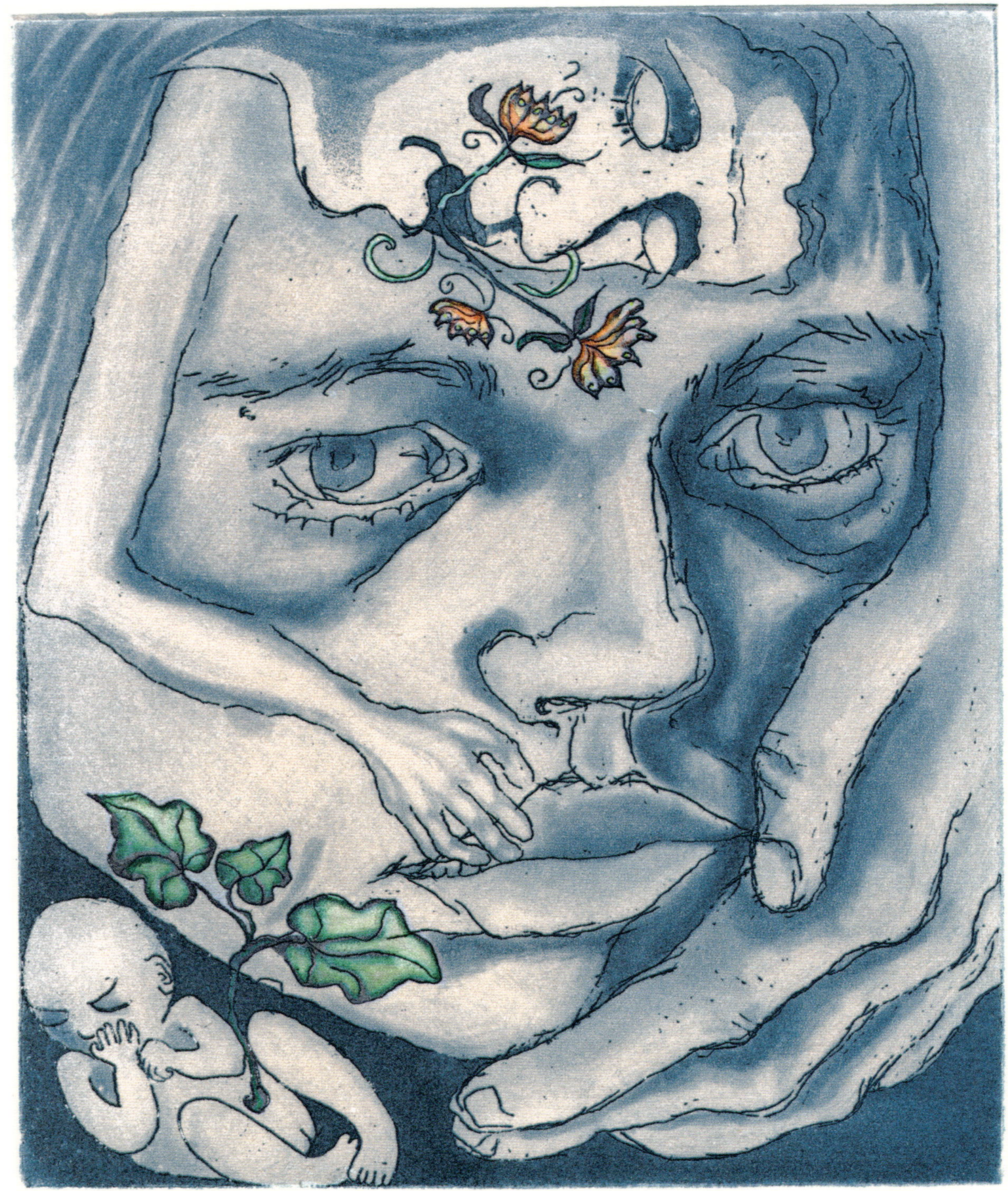

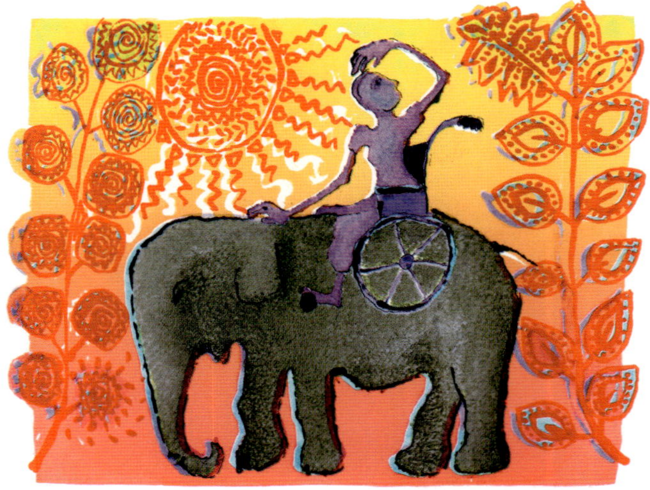

true expression of the lives we were living. In these drawings I wanted to show from within how it feels to be a young woman in a wheelchair.

These works led to a series of images that set out to challenge the prevailing stereotypes about disability; and found their place in the newly emerging disability pride and civil rights movements of the early 1980s.

Around the same time I first encountered Frida Kahlo's works. I was captivated. For the first time in my life I was looking at personal and unashamed representations of a Disabled woman and artist. But I saw more than this. I saw a painter who could express the passion and pain of her personal history with a fierce honesty. In my own work I began to find a voice for the fears and grief, which sometimes threatened to immobilise me more profoundly than my physical impairment.

In my late twenties I had discovered that, contrary to the belief with which I had been brought up, I could live beyond middle age, even into old age. As a child with muscular dystrophy, I had always been told that I would die young. I became haunted by regret that ten years earlier I had undergone an abortion and sterilisation in the belief that I would not live long enough to care for my child who may also inherit my disability.

Gradually I recognised that instead of trying to push away these feelings and thoughts, I needed to bring this experience into my artwork. It seemed that I could only make sense of my life as an artist, if I included everything that mattered to me. By telling my own story I hope to touch on the joys and sorrows we all share.

As a Disabled person I have needed help and support in my life. But through my work as a teacher, and in my relationships I have sought to maintain equality: to find a balance between the giving and receiving of care.

In making artworks I have found a sense of freedom and adventure – those values that I have treasured since my childhood.

I would like to acknowledge and thank Colin Hambrook, Joe McConnell and Allan Sutherland, whose writings about my work have inspired this essay. I would also like to thank Katalin Trencsényi for her editorial advice and assistance.

www.nancywillis.co.uk

left: *Self Portrait with Lost Baby,* etching with hand colouring, 18 x 13cm, 1989

above: *The Explorer,* silkscreen print with hand colouring, 20 x 26cm, 1988

Beautiful Progress to Somewhere?

Amanda Cachia

In 2011, the deaf artist and scholar Joseph Grigely wrote an excellent and influential essay, entitled 'Beautiful Progress to Nowhere,' which contributed towards an extensive collection of commissioned texts compiled and edited by Aaron Williamson for the journal, *Parallel Lines.* The online journal was facilitated and hosted by the Serpentine Gallery in London and funded by Arts Council England.[1] In the text, Grigely talked of how *'there are no easy answers about disability, and no easy answers for Disabled artists. We make progress where we can, even beautiful progress to nowhere, straight into a wall.'*[2] Grigely was making reference to a work by artist Stephen Lapthisophon, which formed part of his solo show at Gallery 400 at the University of Illinois in 2002, entitled 'Within Reasonable Accommodation.'[3]

Lapthisophon had created a bright green-coloured wheelchair ramp, leaned up against a wall, and Grigely used this as an analogy and metaphor for the ambiguous state of the disability legislation around the Americans with Disabilities Act (ADA) of 1990, and the continued obstacles (or walls) faced by artists in securing *'reasonable accommodation'.*

I use Grigely's essay to turn his complex statement into a question – has Disability Arts, indeed, made beautiful progress to nowhere, certainly since Grigely wrote his essay, but also more broadly in the 20th and 21st centuries? The word constraints of this essay mean that I won't be able to explore this question as fully as I might hope, but I would like to offer some reflections and ideas regarding my experiences with *'international'* Disability Arts in the past five years. Much of my thinking wholeheartedly agrees with many of the points that Grigely makes about the many roadblocks that Disabled artists and disability politics continue to face, although I would like to suggest that this *'nowhere'* might be shifted, albeit subtly, towards *'somewhere'*, concluding with a question mark, to indicate that this is an open-ended, yet contentious conversation.

As an Australian woman living and working in California, USA, who identifies as physically Disabled according to the Social Model of Disability, I am often asked for my opinion on the state of Disability Arts in various countries,

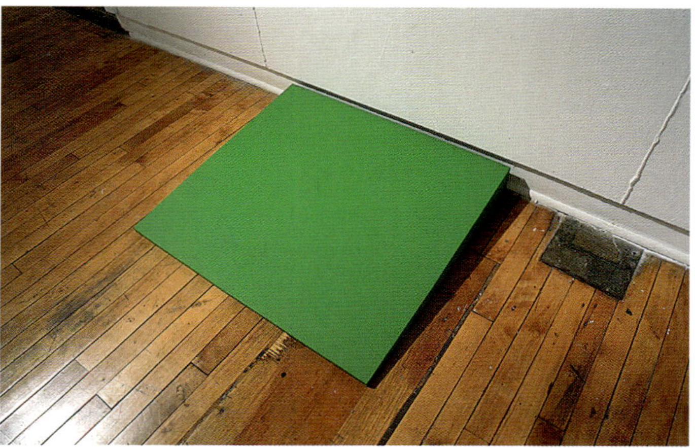

above: Stephen Lapthisophon, *Ramp*, Painted wood, 61 x 10 x 91.5cm, 2002. Photograph Stephen Lapthisophon

specifically that of Australia, Canada, the UK, and the USA (indeed, I cannot speak of the state of Disability Arts outside of these places owing to my limited contact). My response to this question typically suggests that I feel that public arts funding towards disability-based creative initiatives in both the UK, Canada and Australia is quite robust, with the UK at the forefront and as the clear leader in this regard. One thinks of organisations such as Shape Arts in London, DASH in Shrewsbury, Arts Access Australia as Australia's peak body for the arts (along with many other smaller disability-arts organisations throughout its various states), and Tangled Art + Disability based in Toronto as the Canadian counterpart. On the other hand, the USA tends to excel at offering rigorous academic opportunities in disability studies (although not strictly Disability Arts), and the Society for Disability Studies is very active at staging annual conferences and publishing its peer-reviewed journal, *Disability Studies Quarterly.*

Whilst there are few departments dedicated wholly to disability studies in various universities and colleges (Ohio State University and University at Buffalo are some examples), disability studies invariably pops up as a minor subject, housed within other humanities-based academic departments.[4]

My response to this question only truly scratches the surface of the representation, growth and development of 'Disability Arts', for it also arguably encompasses a very narrow definition of what it might come to mean. For example, another facet might consist of the proliferation of Disabled models who are now achieving great national and international success on the world stage and are working to challenge normative and deeply ingrained aesthetic ideals, such as Madeline Stuart, Nyle DiMarco, and Rebekah Marine, who embody Down's Syndrome, deafness and amputee form in that order. In other words, 'Disability Art' has proliferated across the globe in ways beyond the purely visual, where its representation can be experienced in all art forms including theatre, dance, music, architecture, new media, poetry, curatorial studies, and creative writing.

Pedagogically, a number of scholars have also developed handbooks, offering templates for how to teach Disability Arts in the classroom, such as Petra Kuppers and Alice Fox and Hannah Macpherson.[5] Conferences and symposia on 'Disability Arts' have also blossomed, including the current 2016 'Cripping the Arts' conference that recently took place in Toronto thanks to Tangled Art + Disability, not to mention DASH's own 'Awkward Bastards' held at mac Birmingham in 2015. Disability Arts festivals are also flourishing: DaDaFest in Liverpool continues to remain strong, while the brand new US counterpart, DisArt, based in Grand Rapids, Michigan is leading the charge for a new quality and branding of experience for visitors to engage in the vibrancy that is Disability Arts, officially launched in 2015 and securing significant national arts funding through the National Endowment for the Arts.

The world of athleticism and sports has also launched substantial artistic and funding opportunities for 'Disability Arts', such as the *Unlimited* programming that stemmed from the

Olympics and Paralympics in London in 2012, and the PanAm and ParaPanAm Games in Toronto in 2015.

'Disability Arts' also encompasses politics and activism around access, and accommodation. Myself, along with several self-identifying Disabled colleagues at institutions like the University of California Berkeley, including Georgina Kleege, an independent artist Carmen Papalia, are especially interested in issues of 'creative access', where we aim to disseminate and illustrate evolving radical and transgressive ideas in curatorial design for how museum and gallery workers might become competent in building and delivering accessible multi-media practices in museums. We consider innovation in curatorial practice that advances the goal of increasing access to exhibitions by people with sensory, cognitive and physical disabilities. Considering accessible design principles for a wide-range of bodies is critical for the future direction of *all* modalities of design.

For my own part, in terms of attempting to make a contribution towards 'Disability Arts', I am currently working on my PhD dissertation, and my research and scholarship is broadly based at the intersection of contemporary art, the politics of space, and disability studies, where I seek to explore how various Disabled artists and their corresponding audience members engage with the architectures of public space, ranging from the museum to the street; issues that have never before been addressed in art history and criticism. By focusing specifically on aspects of performance, vision and sound, exhibition design, socially engaged, discursive art practice and everyday urban architectures through the work of contemporary Disabled artists, I aim to build a new discourse for the phenomenology of the Disabled spectator. Much of my methodological research over the past few years has also revolved around my curatorial projects with Disabled artists based in Canada and the USA.

The themes and ideas that developed in my exhibitions have also been the source of my overall scholarly writing and thinking, including any outcomes evaluated through visitor attendance and feedback.[6]

Despite all this *'somewhere'* – progress that is occurring – which suggests that the voice of disability and Disabled artists is becoming much louder, more prolific and noticeable than several decades ago, many of us in disability communities still face ongoing 'walls' or barriers within our daily lives. The world was not built for Disabled people, and this fact continues to remain true. We also wrestle with challenging terms and definitions, and this is especially wrapped up with the d-word itself ('d' for 'disability'): which persistently presents a ghettoising conundrum for artists and arts workers alike, who often have to carefully and strategically consider the vicissitudes of self-identification in relation to their complex embodiment, or even their politics, no matter how earnest and strong.[7]

This past winter, 2016, New York-based artist and wheelchair user Park McArthur staged her first solo exhibition in London entitled *Poly*, at the Chisenhale Gallery[8]. McArthur's installation explored *'what it is to bear, to accommodate and to cushion…and the inseparable material*

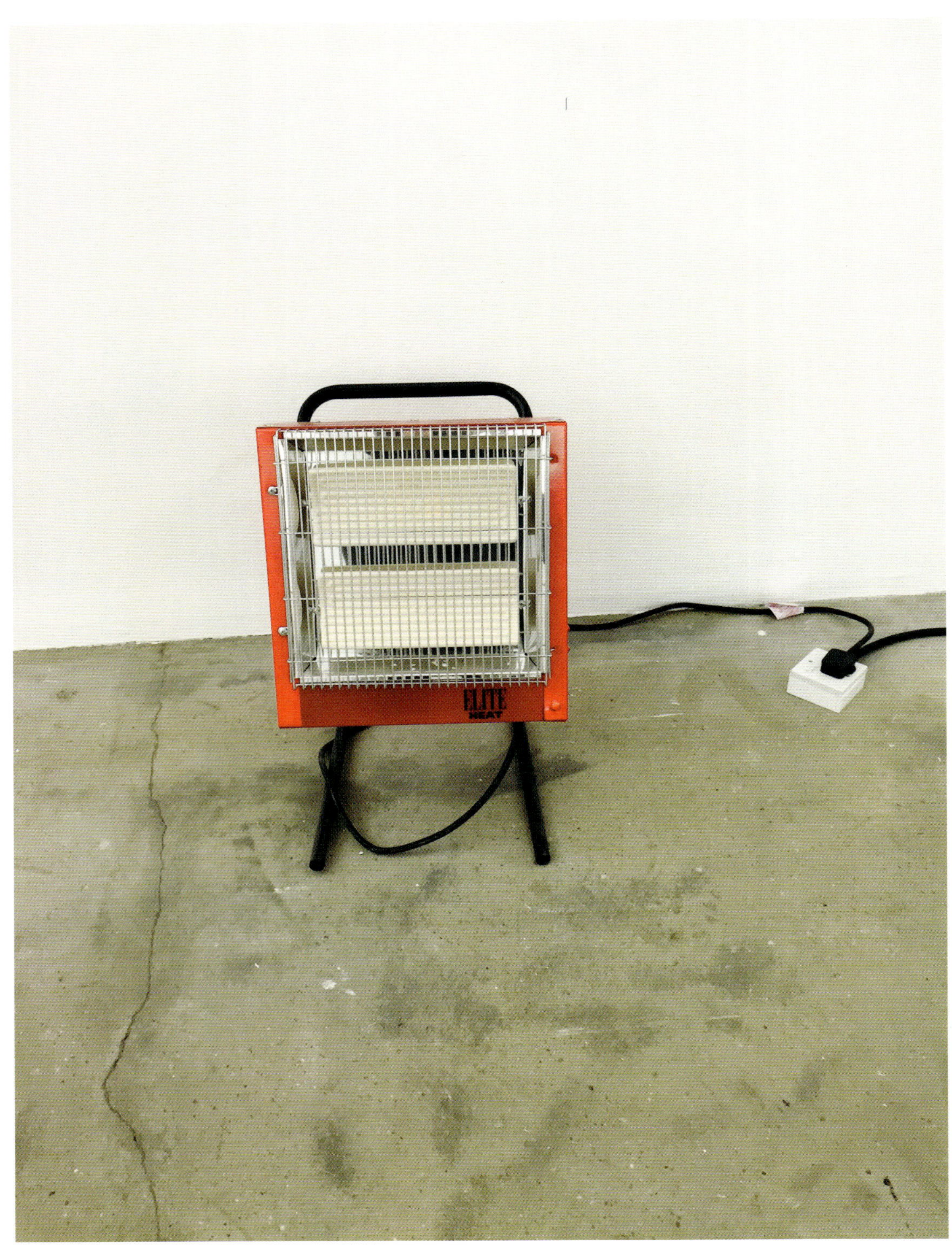

left: Park McArthur, heaters that were included in Poly, 2016, Chisenhale Gallery, London, (not an official artwork, but an accommodation).

relations of art to life.'[9] One unofficial aspect of the exhibition was a series of welcoming red heaters that lay equally spread out around the perimeter of the rectangular box-shaped room.

The heaters were ordered before the installation in order to support the comfort of the artist during her time in the gallery – indeed, they functioned as a subtle, if ambiguous, accommodation, as visitors often easily confused the heaters for actual works of art. If the heaters had not been in the space, then it would not have been possible for the artist to be there on a daily basis as she prepared her show, owing to the unsuitable temperature conditions of the space. The artist had made the decision to keep the heaters as part of her overall installation in order to leave this trace of her individuated existence in the space, but also to keep the space warm for the comfort of her visitors. The heaters act as a tangible accommodation for McArthur's body and that of the audience, and also reveal much about the gallery's intangible engagement with care, demonstrating how the social and atmospheric space of the gallery created its own aesthetic objects through need and desire, where context and effect inform one another. Indeed, through the inclusion of these objects, McArthur provokes us to consider questions around the boundaries between accommodation and art – when is an accommodation an art, and can and is art accommodating?

McArthur's 2016 heaters might also work as a companion to Lapthisophon's 2002 ramp – although rather than an unaccommodating ramp leading to nowhere, in McArthur's show the heaters invite us to share in a space together, embracing accommodation to its utmost potential. These heaters remind us that all our bodies are mapped onto space, even if some of those bodies require more, or different, accommodation than others. McArthur's show is significant for it might act as an antithesis to *'nowhere'* or walls that shut everything down. Instead, it suggests an opening that spans physical, conceptual and dialogic qualities, which also points to how Disability Arts might be *'somewhere'* after all.

1 For more information, see www.parallellinesjournal.com Accessed April 26, 2016

2 www.parallellinesjournal.com/article-beautiful-progress-nowhere.html – Accessed April 26, 2016

3 For more information on the exhibition, visit http://gallery400.uic.edu/exhibitions/with-reasonable-accommodation – Accessed June 1, 2016

4 For a full listing, see http://disabilitystudies.syr.edu/programs-list/ Accessed April 29, 2016

5 For more information, see Petra Kuppers, *Studying Disability Arts and Culture: An Introduction* (New York: Palgrave Macmillan, 2014), and Alice Fox and Hannah Macpherson, *Inclusive Arts Practice and Research: A Critical Manifesto* (New York and London: Routledge, 2015).

6 For more information on some of my projects, visit http://fleshoftheworld.ca/ http://exhibits.haverford.edu/whatcanabodydo/, http://cjds.uwaterloo.ca/index.php/cjds/issue/view/7/showToc

7 For more information on the ghettoisation of disability, see Aaron Williamson's essay, 'In the Ghetto? A Polemic in Place of an Editorial' in *Parallel Lines* journal, http://www.parallellinesjournal.com/article-in-the-ghetto.html Accessed April 26, 2016

8 For more information on this exhibition, visit http://www.chisenhale.org.uk/archive/exhibitions/index.php?id=177 – Accessed June 1, 2016

9 http://www.chisenhale.org.uk/archive/exhibitions/index.php?id=177 – Accessed April 26, 2016

Dedication and thanks

This book is dedicated to Disabled artists everywhere, without whose passion, commitment and vibrant work it would have been not only meaningless, but impossible.

Due to the limitations imposed by the size of the book, there are many Disabled artists whose work we have been unable to include on this occasion, but whose diverse work makes up the essential web that is Disability Art.

We would like to thank the following people and organisations for their contributions to making the book possible:

The contributing artists, for sharing their artistic journeys in words and images.

Darren Henley OBE, Chief Executive Officer (ACE) contributed his opening comments;

Abid Hussain, Director Diversity (ACE) gave his ongoing support, and advocated the importance of the publication.

The authors, Craig Ashley, former Producer at mac Birmingham, now Director at New Art West Midlands, Amanda Cachia, Disabled Curator and academic (USA/Australia) and Tony Heaton OBE, Chief Executive Officer of Shape and a Disabled artist, for their illuminating essays, which give the book its energy and tone.

aquarium graphic design ltd., mac Birmingham, Lois Keidan at LADA, Kaye Winwood Projects and Clare Nankivell – for all their support and guidance.

The DASH staff – Mike Layward, Artistic Director; Paula Dower, Operations Director and Carrie Slawinska, Administration Assistant – for their ongoing enthusiasm and hard work on the project.

Tanya Raabe-Webber, artist, and Adrian Plant, curator, have edited the book, and deserve our gratitude for their hard work and tenacity.

References

DASH www.dasharts.org

Shape www.shapearts.org.uk

Disability Arts Online DAO
www.disabilityarts.online and their Directory
http://disabilityarts.online/directory/

DaDa Fest www.dadafest.co.uk

Unlimited www.weareunlimited.org.uk

Project Ability www.project-ability.co.uk

Outside In www.outsidein.org.uk

The Arthouse www.the-arthouse.org.uk

Disability Arts Cymru DAC
www.dacymru.com

Arts and Disability Forum Northern Ireland
www.adf.ie

Arts and Disability Ireland www.adiarts.ie